CARLISLE'S SUBURBS SERIES

Denton Holme

Denis Perriam

A catalogue record for this book is available from the British Library

ISBN 978-0-9931835-7-7

Copyright © Denis Perriam 2019

Published by:
P3 Publications
13 Beaver Road
Carlisle
Cumbria
CA2 7PS

Printed by:
Gomer Press
Llandysul Enterprise Park
Ceredigion
SA44 4JL

Above: St James Church from the architect's drawing of 1865 in the *Carlisle Patriot,* Carlisle Library.

Opposite: this holy water stoup is one of the few archaeological finds from Denton Holme. Originally on Seven Wells Bank it is now inside St James Church.

INTRODUCTION

Few historians had taken an interest in Denton Holme until a two-part study written by Roy Hudleston and Alan Harris, was published in the *Transactions of the Cumberland and Westmorland Antiquarian Society* in 1967 and 1968. There was then a joint exhibition in 1982 organised by the County Record Office and Carlisle Museum on the area, held in the Community Centre. To accompany this a four-page leaflet was produced by Bruce Jones and Sue Kirby summarising the history of Denton Holme.
National recognition came in 1983 when David Waugh featured Sheffield Street in his book, *The British Isles*, as an example of Victorian housing development.

The present author was approached by Joan Inglis in 1991 to produce a brief history of Denton Holme for the Carlisle and District Civic Trust. A prototype A5 14-page booklet was produced but the money to fund the project was not forthcoming. In 1994 the author was commissioned, this time by Peter Messenger, to produce a pictorial record of Denton Holme history to help the City Council with future planning decisions. A copy was placed in the Jackson Library for public consultation but it was never intended for publication. With Babs Cullen's *Denton Holme Childhood* in 1994 came the first book to feature the history of the area. Since then there have been books and booklets which have concentrated on one particular Denton Holme industry. Where appropriate those books are featured here.
The time had come to bring all of the information together in one volume and while the above publications have been a valuable source there are subjects for which no previous research had been done; for that reason there will be some gaps. Every effort has been made to cover every diverse aspect of the history of Denton Holme in an easy to read form.

ACKNOWLEDGEMENTS

As with the previous book in this series Mary Scott-Parker generously offered to type the original draft. Photography was undertaken by Findlay Stirling, Barry Beckett and Dennis Irwin and thanks are given for their skills. Stephen White has been of great help in locating obscure facts and illustrations. John Huggon has read the text offering additional information and corrections. Thanks are given to those organisations who have provided archive pictures; Carlisle Library, the Archive Centre, Tullie House Museum and Art Gallery Trust and others who are individually acknowledged. Private collectors have been of help and particular thanks are given to Ashley Kendall, David Young and Bill Boak. Every effort has been made to contact copyright holders but anyone overlooked should contact the publishers.

INDEX

ORIGINS

John Robinson

Left: Civil War earthworks west of the city during the 1644-45 siege included one at Murrell Hill.

On 5 May 1645 Isaac Tullie wrote in his diary, ".... the roundheads brought a number of countrey labourers to raise a work on Morall hill who were soe cannonered from the Castle that they run all away; yet afterwards they finished it..."

Above: the Denton coat-of-arms

Predating Denton ownership, Murrell is the oldest place name element in the holme.

A holme is defined as "Any piece of land isolated from its surroundings", and in Denton Holme this probably related to the area between the river and the millrace. Later the name applied to a larger landmass.

Henry I, 1100 - 1135, granted to Morvin part of the manor of Shaddongate which included Denton Holme. Morvin's son, Hervey, inherited giving this the name Hervey Holme.

He then gave the land to Gwery the Fleming on his marriage to Hervey's daughter Muriel, hence the name Murrell Hill. By 1283 Denton Holme became part of the Gerbot lands and in 1383 was sold to the Denton family who held this until selling off the last part in 1680.

Above: the street name of this part of Dalston Road was originally Murrell Hill.

Below: much of Murrell Hill remained undeveloped as shown in this late 1940s view from Dixon's factory.

Denis Perriam two images

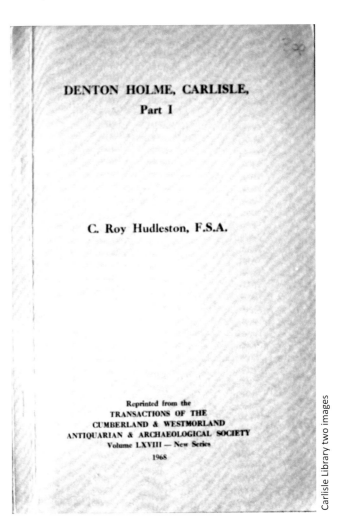

DENTON HOLME, CARLISLE,
Part I

C. Roy Hudleston, F.S.A.

Reprinted from the
TRANSACTIONS OF THE
CUMBERLAND & WESTMORLAND
ANTIQUARIAN & ARCHAEOLOGICAL SOCIETY
Volume LXVIII — New Series
1968

Carlisle Library two images

Above: Roy Hudleston wrote about the medieval history and part two by Alan Harris dealt with the 19th century development.

ROMANS

Right: this red sandstone tombstone was probably found at the same time as the one opposite but was not immediately recognised. When it was given to Carlisle Museum the *Carlisle Journal* in July 1881 reported it "was found in excavating for the extension of James Nelson's marble works."

The photograph was taken by James Dennison before it was given to the museum. The catalogue describes this as being "a boat with a mast and standing rigging," at the top. "Below is the upper part of a figure of Hercules, who is clad in a lion-skin and grasps a large club in both hands." It may represent Hercules leaving the Argo in quest of the missing Hylas.

Above: gravestone of the woman with a fan and child found in 1878 at Murrell Hill. This was described as "the most elaborate example of funeray sculpture so far discovered in Carlisle.

Below: Reconstruction made in 1958 to show the woman above.

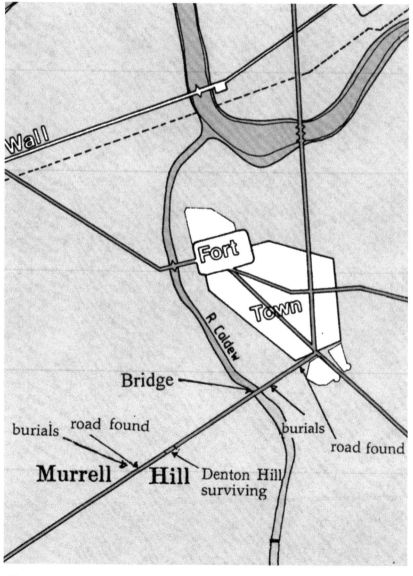

Above: map showing the projected route of Roman roads around Carlisle.

Peter W Robinson

Left: the siding on the right into the former Nelson's marble works where the railway cutting was made in 1879 and the Roman road was found. James Nelson had relocated here because of the construction of the Viaduct and the rail connection from the Canal Branch was important for the delivery of heavy blocks of stone. As a sculptor Nelson appreciated the importance of the carved Roman stones found here.

Roman law forbade burials within towns so these were usually along the roads leading in and out, where they would be prominent especially on a hillside. In November 1879 RS Ferguson stated that at Murrell Hill a "road has been found in the excavating of a railway cutting into Mr Nelson's premises - a paved road, over 30 feet wide, with ditches at each side". This he thought "must be the great Roman road from Roman Carlisle to the west and by its direction it must have left Carlisle at the spot where was afterwards the English Gate." Some finds were made nearby, "an interment in a cist of thin slabs...and also some pottery." This was near to where the carved stone of the lady and child had been found and also the Hercules tombstone.

The road was a continuation of the one from Thursby which followed a straight line through Morton Park and Murrell Hill; it was also found close to the gaol wall and Victoria Viaduct. Funerary objects were found in the Caledonian Railway goods yard in 1862 close to where the road would have crossed the Caldew.

Denis Perriam two images

Above: blockwork in the bed of the river where a Roman bridge would have been necessary to carry the road into Carlisle.

Left: the street, Denton Hill, now the entrance into Longhorn, is on the line of the Roman road.

RIVER CALDEW

Carlisle Library

Above: the Vale of Caldew viewed from Cummersdale in a 1832 lithograph by Matthew Nutter.

Findlay Stirling

Above: flood prevention work with walls and gates has been carried out since the 2005 floods which helped prevent the deluge of 2015 doing any damage to Denton Holme.

The river originates in the Caldbeck Fells and was not only a source of water but a means of powering machinery. This combined with the fact that from the rocks the water passed through it acquired certain properties which helped in bleaching cloth, in the days before chemical bleach, made this a place of industrial development.

Given the name by Romantics, the Vale of Caldew, this was used in place names during the Victorian period.

With the volume of water coming down from the mountains there was always the risk of flooding.

Denis Perriam

Above: this stretch of the Caldew provided a rich source of gravel for local builders.

Below: the effects of the 2005 flood on Denton Street.

David Ramshaw

DENTON HOLME MILLRACE

Left: the 1864 dam replaced earlier ones at Holme Head and a sluice below the railings regulates the water entering the millrace which flowed through the Ferguson Bros buildings behind.

Below: annotated map showing the millrace and the associated factory buildings.

A dam must have existed at Holme Head in the medieval period because there are early references to mills which could not have existed without the Denton Holme millrace.

From the dam across the River Caldew, a watercourse was cut through Denton Holme and Shaddongate, flowing back into the river at Willow Holme. For years there were only two corn mills on its course, but in the 18th century textile mills rapidly developed along the millrace. When water became less important as a source of power and factories turned to steam, the route of the millrace could be traced by the factory chimneys.

Few industries now use water from the millrace and although minor changes have been made to its course, its future seems assured as it controls the volume of water flowing through the main channel of the river in times of flood.

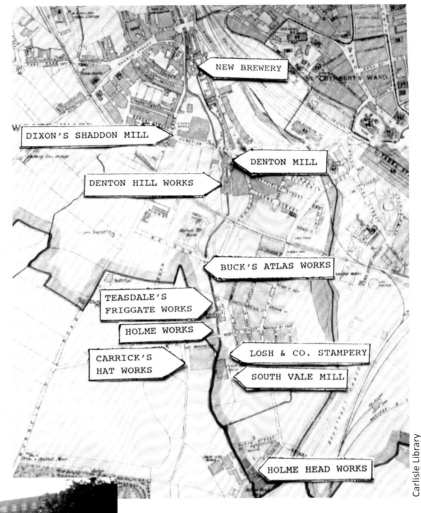

NEW BREWERY

DIXON'S SHADDON MILL

DENTON MILL

DENTON HILL WORKS

BUCK'S ATLAS WORKS

TEASDALE'S FRIGGATE WORKS

HOLME WORKS

LOSH & CO. STAMPERY

CARRICK'S HAT WORKS

SOUTH VALE MILL

HOLME HEAD WORKS

Carlisle Library

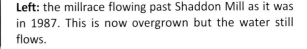

Denis Perriam two images

Left: the millrace flowing past Shaddon Mill as it was in 1987. This is now overgrown but the water still flows.

HOLME HEAD WORKS

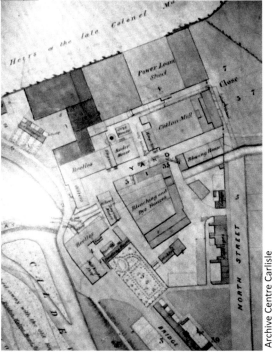

John Huggon

Left: an advertising lithograph of the factory buildings about 1900.

Below: original coloured plan of the works at Holme Head earlier than the lithograph showing the uses of all the different buildings.

Archive Centre Carlisle

The early history of Holme Head works is not easily understood. An advert in the *Carlisle Journal* 31 May 1817 gives the bankruptcy of "William Bentley and Joshua Ireland of Denton Holme Head, cotton spinners." On 1 May 1819 the newspaper offered for sale "The cotton twist mill at Holme Head newly erected…. now in the occupation of Messrs Ritson & Lemon." Later the newspaper stated "there was another water-powered cotton mill at Holme Head of three stories, a narrow white building, which [in 1886] still remains standing. In this building cotton spinning was carried on up to about 1820," and this seems to be the early works. It was taken by Carrick, Johnston & Co who moved to Dalston. The premises were taken by Joseph Ferguson in 1828.

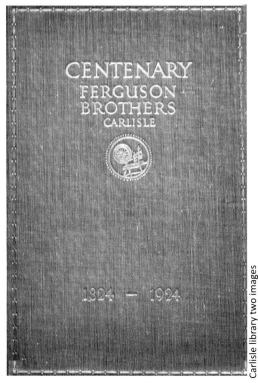

Ferguson Centenary Book

Left: miniature portrait of Joseph Ferguson by TH Carrick. Ferguson was the founder of the firm.

Right: history of the firm written in 1924 to mark the centenary of Ferguson Brothers. This gives much detail of those involved in the management and history of the firm.

Carlisle library two images

Above: some of Ferguson Bros fabrics on display in 1958.

Above: bales of raw cotton being handled at the works in 1958, this coming from Egypt.

Below: the *Cumberland News* headline 6 September 1991.

Ferguson had worked in his father's textile firm but "in 1824 he left to commence business on his own account as a dyer and finisher of cotton goods at the Friggate Works." There he beetled cloth to produce a high finish and was successful enough by 1828 to rent "a mill at Holme Head previously occupied by Messrs Carrick & Johnston, cotton spinners."

In 1837 an entire new set of factory buildings were erected for Ferguson.

In 1865 it was decided to bring all the processes of the production of finished cloth on the Holme Head site with a spinning mill and weaving sheds. As input increased larger buildings were needed and older ones demolished. The last large extension of the works was between 1920 and 1921.

200 jobs hit by shutdown

Ferguson print firm gets chop

A CARLISLE textile company is to close with the loss of 200 jobs.

Ferguson Printers in Holme Head made the shock announcement late yesterday afternoon.

Bosses blamed cheap foreign imports and the recession.

Many large textile firms in Carlisle were taken over and Ferguson Bros was no exception becoming part of the Carrington Viyella Group as Ferguson Printers. A decision was taken in 1991 to close the factory this being attributed to "the recession and cheap foreign imports." Parts of the works were demolished but larger buildings were saved to be converted into luxury flats.

Left: factory buildings remain at Holme Head but now put to other uses. The manager's house was more recently a pub but plans to make this into a school came to nothing.

Above: a works magazine was produced for many years with a title which reflected the location.

LOSH & CO

Denis Perriam

Left: the stampery buildings in the early 19th century. These consisted of "large convenient printing shops, dyeing house and drying house" covering one acre and 18 acres of bleachfields.

The firm of Losh, James and Co is listed in 1775 as "calico printers at Denton Holme." It seems this was the same business with different partners in 1783; Thomas Benson, George Mounsey, Thomas Losh, John Milbourne and John Wasdale, trading as "Losh & Co, Denton Holme."

A map of the same year shows the ownership as 'Milbourne's Stampery' another contemporary map giving the same building with the tenant's name 'Losh & Co Cotton Stampery'. One of those apprenticed there was the Cumberland bard, Robert Anderson.

As partners died or withdrew they were replaced and in 1797 George Blamire and Richard Tyson were additional partners. Others to join were JM Dixon and Anthony Holmes who died in 1812. The founding partner, Thomas Losh, died in 1811 but the company continued in his name. The mill had been Milbourne property but it passed to the Dixons who offered it for sale as the lease was up for renewal. There was no buyer in 1819 so Losh & Co renewed the lease with a new partnership of brothers, William, Thomas and John Losh trading from 1821.

They continued until being declared bankrupt in 1841 when the mill was again for sale. The unoccupied buildings were finally sold in 1852.

DENTON HOLME PRINT WORKS
Near Carlisle, to be Sold or Let.

TO be SOLD, by PRIVATE CONTRACT, or LET, for such a Term of Years as may be agreed upon, with immediate possession, all those Buildings, formerly occupied by Messrs. LOSH, as PRINT WORKS, situate near the City of Carlisle and known by the name of the DENTON HOLME PRINT WORKS.

Also, TWO CLOSES or INCLOSURES of LAND, situate near the above, containing 14 Acres, or thereabouts, of excellent Land, which will be Sold or Let together with or separately from the Print Works, at the option of the Purchaser or Tenant.

The Premises have a constant Supply of Water, with a powerful fall, and are well adapted for Print Works, or for Manufacturing purposes. The Owners will thoroughly repair them for an eligible Tenant. There is a Coal Depôt in the immediate neighbourhood. Mrs. DIXON, Holme Foot, will send a person to show the Property; and for further particulars apply to her or Messrs. MOUNSEY and MC. ALPIN, Solicitors, Carlisle.

Carlisle, Sept. 30, 1851.

Above: sale notice for what had originally been Losh & Co in the *Carlisle Journal* 11 October 1851.

Below: a receipt for the reformed firm of 1821. Most Carlisle textile businesses had an office in Manchester as well.

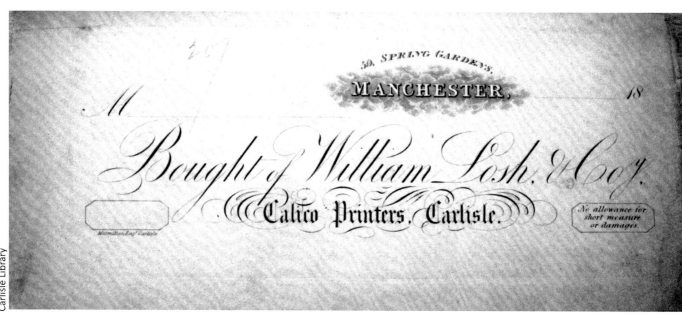

Carlisle Library

SOUTH VALE MILL

John Huggon/Vince White

The former Losh & Co site was sold on 29 May 1852 by John Milbourne Dixon to Joseph Rome who had the old buildings demolished. Plans by J Hogg in 1853 show a "corn mill, three houses, stables, piggeries, etc… with a water wheel for Joseph Rome." The *Carlisle Journal* reported in December 1853 that the mill was let to Carr's, "the buildings have been constructed by Messrs Nelson and will shortly be in operation." With improvements for steam machinery Carr's remained until the opening of an improved Silloth flour mill in 1904. South Vale Mill was then offered for sale but there was no taker and shortly afterwards the mill buildings were demolished. What remained of the buildings along Leicester Street were used for various purposes and from 1952 as a distribution depot by Carlisle Milk Distributors (and the Co-op) until eventual demolition to be replaced by housing.

Top: milk tokens used by the company operating South Vale as their depot.

Above: Carr's advert showing South Vale Mill when this was their flour mill.

Below left: demolition of the remaining buildings in 1990. Below: the sale notice in 1905.

Bill Boak

CARLISLE.
The South Vale Mill.

To be Sold by Auction
IN THE
County Estate Auction Rooms,
31 Lowther Street, Carlisle,
ON
MONDAY, JANUARY 23rd, 1905,
At 3 o'clock in the Afternoon precisely.

Archive Centre Carlisle

CARRICK'S

Denis Perriam

Left: the 1877 buildings on Norfolk Street, with extensions, continued in use until demolition in 2005.

Below: the 1900 OS map showing the extent of the works alongside the Denton Holme millrace.

Bottom left: one of the silk labels which would be placed in the lining of a bowler or top hat.
Bottom: examples of hats made by Carricks.

Founded in the 1770s by William Carrick, Carrick's Hattery was at first in English Damside, moving to a site in Wapping. There were a number of hat manufacturers in Carlisle but Carricks relied on the quality of their products and they were soon leaders in the market for top and bowler hats.

When extensions were proposed for the Citadel Station in 1876 the Carrick site was required and with compensation the firm was able to relocate to Denton Holme. The new factory at South Vale was ready in December 1877.

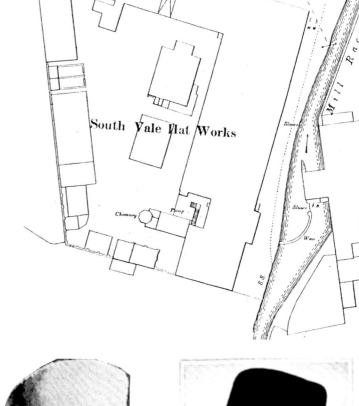

South Vale Hat Works

Carlisle Library four images

14

KANGOL

Left: a child seat restraint from a 1976 advert.

Right: this 1971 advert shows that by then Kangol was a major supplier for the motor industry. A new company Auto Restraint Systems Ltd was announced in February 1971 jointly owned by Kangol and Smiths Industries.

THERE'S SAFETY IN OUR NUMBERS

KANGOL HAVE SUPPLIED OVER 12,000,000 SAFETY BELTS AND CRASH HELMETS ALL OVER THE WORLD

Kangol was established at Cleator in 1938 to make berets which became popular in World War Two with the military and civilians - the name coming from **K**nitted **ANG**ora wo**OL**, the principal constituent of berets. The business expanded with a takeover of Carrick's in 1954 where flat cap production continued. Diversification saw experiments with motorcycle helmets made out of injected plastic. This safety element was further expanded to manufacture seat belts for cars in the early 60s. As safety became a legal requirement production increased to make Kangol the leading manufacturer in motor safety accessories.

KANGOL MAGNET
The best seat belt
with the exclusive magnetic buckle
is made here in
CARLISLE

Kangol Magnet Limited, Carlisle
A member of the Kangol Group of Companies

Left: there were various improvements and take-overs which resulted in changes to the company name. This advert comes from 1967.

Right: much more on the history of the firm is given in Alan Tucker's book produced in 2017 taking it through to eventual demise in 2005.
Below: where the factory had been is now occupied by flats appropriately named.

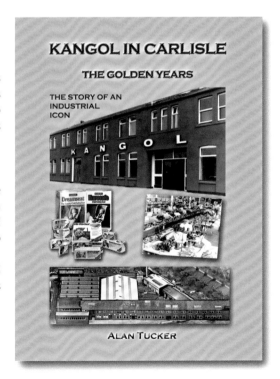

KANGOL IN CARLISLE
THE GOLDEN YEARS
THE STORY OF AN INDUSTRIAL ICON
ALAN TUCKER

KANGOL PLACE

HOLME WORKS

Above: Holme Works on Norfolk Street today.

PARIS.

1878

Above: the medal the company won at the 1878 Paris Exhibition.

Denis Perriam two images

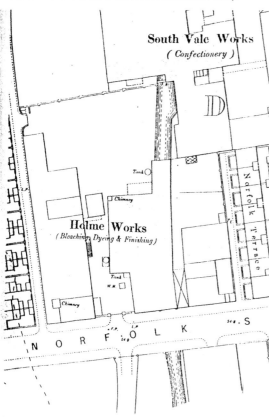

Above: 1900 OS map showing the extent of the works.

Deeds of 27 March 1860 show land on Norfolk Street was bought by brothers-in-law Nathan Palmer and George Story. That year plans were submitted for Holme Works there for the finishing processes of woven cloth. At the International Exhibition of 1862 they showed taffeta, silk and cotton umbrella cloths. Success meant extensions to the works in 1864. Trading as Palmer & Story the firm exhibited at the Paris International Exhibition in 1878, "umbrella fabric, sateens for tailors and dressmakers; Italian cloth and Silesias…. in shades fashionable in Paris - light lavender, light green and light pink."

A split came in 1884 when Nathan Palmer left for Shaddongate Beetling Works and George Story & Sons continued at Holme Works. Story died in 1890 and his sons, Walter and John, continued the business right through World War One, fully employed with military contracts. WP Story died in 1925 and his sons continued making tailors' linings until offering the building for sale in 1949, GC Robinson being the purchaser. Messrs W Wood & Co took part as a joiner's workshop and another part as a bakehouse for the Silver Grill. Various businesses have used the frontage for shops and the bakehouse converted to flats.

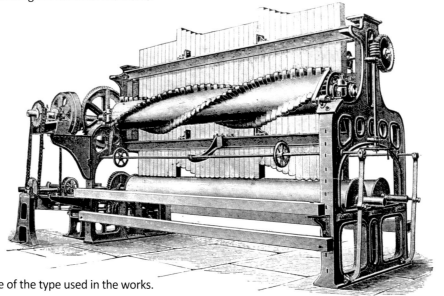

Right: beetling machine of the type used in the works.

Carlisle Library two images

16

FRIGGATE WORKS

Left: the 1899 building along Westmorland Street demolished in 2006.

Below: where the factory had been, housing has been built with appropriate street names.

Bottom left: a worker packing sweets inside the works in 1958.

Bottom right: one of the best-selling products of Teasdale's was the 'Nipits' throat pastille, the company was already using the penguin symbol in 1946.

Denis Perriam two images

TEASDALE PLACE

HOLSTEAD CLOSE

Friggate was a field name and a fulling mill is shown there on a map of 1781, a place where wool was processed after weaving. Later this was named Friggate Works where Joseph Ferguson finished and dyed cotton cloth before his move to Holme Head in 1828. John Thompson then had this as a dyeing and bleaching works until 1858. Thomas Holstead had started business as a confectioner in 1839 and moved this to Friggate Works in 1858. In 1866 Isaac Teasdale came from Little Salkeld as a commission agent for Holstead. When the partnership of Thomas and William Holstead was dissolved in 1870 Teasdale went into partnership with John Craig until 1872 when Teasdale took complete control. When Friggate Works were offered for sale in 1875 the purchaser at £1,400 was Isaac Teasdale the sitting tenant. The firm started with only 25 employees but numbers increased as business expanded. From 1 February 1877 it traded as Isaac Teasdale & Co and was incorporated in June 1898 as a limited company. Additions were made in 1899 with a completely new building fronting Westmorland Street. When Teasdale died in 1914 there was a workforce of 400 and the company continued in his name.

After World War One a new four-storey block was built behind the existing one. The *Carlisle Journal* in 1928 reported "the firm's goods enjoy a fine reputation, not only in this country but also in the Dominions." There was stiff competition after the war and in 1963 Messrs Harridene of London took over changing the name to Penguin Confectionery.

A merger with Carter & Sons of Sheffield resulted in more jobs with more than 400 workers in 1968. In 1999 the company was placed in receivership and in December 2000 it was bought by House of York. They closed the factory in March 2004 and all was replaced by a housing development.

Carlisle Library

JULY, 1946   Copyright. 4d.

NIPITS

VOICE, THROAT & CHEST PASTILLES

2d. per packet

MADE BY
TEASDALE & CO. LTD
OF
CARLISLE

Carlisle & District Bus Timetable 1946

ATLAS WORKS

Carlisle Journal 3 August 1928

Left: the Nelson Street factory.

Below: the Buck trade-mark was Atlas so Nelson Street became the Atlas Works.

Bottom left: JP Buck was the son of RR Buck and became the managing partner.

Bottom right: the cartouche over a doorway in the 1877 part of the building for JA Thomlinson.

The Nelson Street factory was built for textile manufacturer John Ashbridge Thomlinson in 1877. He was bankrupt in 1882 and the building was acquired for £4,000 by the Carlisle and Cumberland Bank.

Robert Robinson Buck, born at Skipton, went into partnership with Joseph Pattinson in 1851 to become Pattinson & Buck. They operated two mills at Dalston and in 1883 they took Thomlinson's factory along with all the machinery, Pattinson dropping out of the partnership. Additions were made in 1896 and the mills at Dalston were closed in 1897 as all production was then centred at Carlisle.

Congregational Church Jubilee Booklet

Denis Perriam two images

Left: the factory interior about 1909.

Middle left: a 1911 catalogue giving details of the different fabrics manufactured.

Bottom left: ladies shirt blouses made by Buck from the 1911 catalogue.

Bottom right: shirts and pyjamas by Bucks also in the catalogue.

Fancy flannel fabrics for fashionable folk.

R.R. BUCK & SONS.
CARLISLE,

Retaining the original name of Messrs RR Buck, although the founder died in 1897, the firm was very successful manufacturing underwear, pyjamas and shirts and at one point employed 500.

Post-war changes were made in 1959 when the weaving department closed, cloth then being bought in. The building was then too large and parts were let to other companies. Border Publicity was the first to take a share in 1960 followed by Hunter's Bakery in 1962. Part of the works was sold to Teasdale's, leading to the closure of Teasdale's Lane. Brown's furniture warehouse came in 1965 and Pirelli in 1966. Former weaving sheds were used by JW Hodgson Transport and Halsteads.

Bucks continued into the 1980s but foreign competition saw an end to production at Nelson Street. Rather than demolition new uses have been found and a number of businesses now use the former factory.

Below: Buck's stand at the Franco-British Exhibition in London, 1908, where the company won an award.

DENTON HILL WORKS

Above: the results of the Denton Hill fire in 1914 and the replacement building on the right dated 1923 and designed by Robert Lorimer.

John Huggon

There was 18th century industry on this site but it is difficult to place a particular firm when documents do not state exactly where they were. By 1809 Robson Clark had a bleach works here which was twice washed away in floods that year and 1811. His buildings were also damaged by fire as were the works of Robert Ferguson at Denton Hill in 1813. Later J & JR Ferguson was at Denton Hill but with John Ferguson dead in 1829 his brother Richard went into partnership with John Chambers but still traded under the Ferguson name. John Chambers formed a new partnership with the Donald brothers trading as John Ferguson & Co. When Chambers died in 1850 the name was changed to Donald Brothers. The brothers decided to discontinue manufacture in 1891 and a new firm of Donald Irlam & Co was formed, but this was short lived. For the latter part of the 1890s a number of different companies used the works until sold to Alexander Morton & Co in 1899. This then became the Morton Sundour factory which when Courtaulds took over in 1963 was used by various subsidiaries. Part became Gleneden Textiles in 1956, which from 1975 specialised in weaving car seat covers.

Courtaulds then sold this in 1997 to Collins & Aikman who ceased manufacture there in 2006. Today the buildings are used by Longhorn Glass.

The remaining weaving sheds were continued as Lappet Manufacturing Co who make the traditional Saudi Arabian shawls, seen left, for export, but redundancies were threatened in 2018.

Cumberland News

Right: Jocelyn Morton wrote the history of the various Morton firms which included Morton Sundour and subsidiaries.

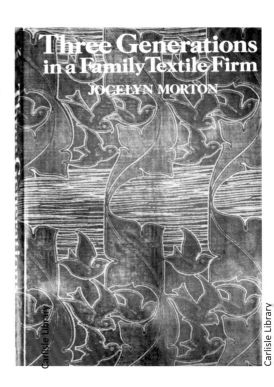

Carlisle Library

MORTON SUNDOUR

Sundour Shuttle June 1938

Sundour Shuttle Dec. 1950

Above: Alexander Morton founder of the firm.

Above left: modernisation continued in 1937 when Morton's built a new office and warehouse in the grounds of Murrell Hill House with an entrance from Nelson Street. The building is seen here in 1938 with Kenmount Place in the background. Today this is the site of the offices for Electricity North West.

Above and right: blocks used by Thurnams to print the company letterheads.

Right: a Morton subsidiary was Edinburgh Weavers which from 1928 was based in the Scottish capital before the fledgling company relocated to Carlisle in 1932. Their address in 1933-4 was given as Lorne Crescent which was the location of the Denton Hill works. Later they gave a London address but all the manufacturing was carried out in Carlisle. In the book Lesley Jackson gives the history of the firm and the modern designs produced by the company. Examples of the products are in the collection of the Victoria & Albert Museum and are illustrated in the book.

Carlisle Library

Sundour Shuttle June 1936

Left: like many other large factories in Carlisle Morton Sundour produced their own works magazine from 1935 to 1957. These are a useful source giving details on the workers and the textiles they manufactured in Carlisle.

SOLWAY DYES CO.

Denis Perriam two images

Left: this was the laboratory built by Morton's in 1918 for Solway Dyes Co, the factory known as Murrell Hill Colour Works being behind this building.

The production of coloured cloth was threatened by war in 1914. Chemical dyes had been developed in Germany and the industry relied on them for 80% of our dyes. Using German patents from the Patent Office James Morton employed chemists to produce blue and yellow vat dyes at Carlisle to supply the factory by 27 March 1915. Not only did Morton Sundour manufacture substitutes for German dyes in quantity they also produced new colours. Many of these products were protected by patents taken out by Morton's.

To enable the production of the chemical dyes a new factory had to be built on a site on Lorne Crescent. Under the name of Solway Dyes Co, Murrell Hill Colour Works produced in 1919 half of the total pre-war British consumption of dyestuffs. The confined site made it impossible to expand so the company relocated in the 1920s.

Sundour Shuttle Dec.1938

Above: the surviving dye works chimney on Lorne Crescent along with the brick wall of the main factory buiding, now covered in metal cladding.

Left: James Morton (later knighted) was the driving force behind the replacement of German dyes.

HADRIAN MILL

Carlisle Library two images

Left: the new mill viewed from Atlas Works looking over Blencowe Street in 1969.

Below: the control room in the new factory with Sheila Thomlinson behind the desk.

Courtaulds took over Morton Sundour in 1963 and saw potential in Carlisle but modernisation was needed. Work began in 1967 in clearing a site in the former Murrell Hill gardens. A completely new factory, Hadrian Mill was built on the site in 1968 as part of Courtaulds Northern Weaving Division. This was equipped with state of art machinery. A 1969 advert stated that the mill "now employs 500 and provides fabric for all parts of the world".

Changes in the market for textiles with foreign competition meant that the plant closed in the early 1980s with a loss of 350 jobs. The building was then acquired by NORWEB and after extensive adaptation it became their Hadrian Depot opened by Lord Whitelaw in June 1986. Redundant to United Utilities requirements the building was demolished in 2016.

Right: the weaving machines inside Hadrian Mill when new.

Below: fabric woven at Hadrian Mill.

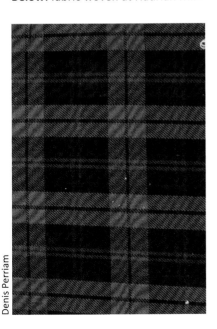

Denis Perriam

Harold Benson

DENTON MILL

Tullie House Museum and Art Gallery Trust

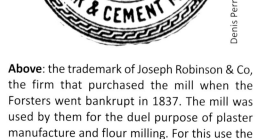

Denis Perriam

Above: the trademark of Joseph Robinson & Co, the firm that purchased the mill when the Forsters went bankrupt in 1837. The mill was used by them for the duel purpose of plaster manufacture and flour milling. For this use the mill was rebuilt in 1834.

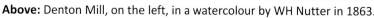

Above: Denton Mill, on the left, in a watercolour by WH Nutter in 1863.

This had been a medieval water-corn mill powered by the Denton Holme millrace. Various documents refer to the mill particularly when land was being sold by the Denton family in the 17th century, this being one of the few buildings in the area.

In one of the sales the mill became the property of the Forster family.

Cumberland News

Michael Davies-Shiel

Denton Mill was taken by Carr's as a flour mill when Robinsons decided to cease biscuit and flour manufacture in the 1860s.
They used the mill until 1885 when flour milling was transferred to Silloth. The building was then bought by the South End Coop and they rebuilt in 1886.

Left: the rebuilt Coop mill on the corner of Junction Street and Lorne Crescent [previously Milbourne Crescent]. The rear of the building [left] faced the millrace. After having been derelict since the mid 1960s the building was demolished in the 1970s.

SHADDON MILL

Carlisle library two images

Above: Peter Dixon was born at Whitehaven and came to Warwick Bridge in 1807 as a partner in Langthwaite Mill run by his Ferguson brothers-in-law. He became managing partner in 1814.

The firm of Peter Dixon & Sons relocated to a purpose-built spinning mill on Junction Street in 1836. This was designed by Richard Tattersall with a tall chimney. Weaving was off-site and gradually the mill was expanded to include weaving machinery. The firm faced bankruptcy in 1872 and was reformed as Peter Dixon & Sons Ltd., but this only lasted until final bankruptcy in 1883. All the machinery and buildings were sold. Robert Todd & Sons then took Shaddon Mill and shared part with Solric D'Fyson Fabrics Ltd. The weaving shed became Linton Tweeds.

Todds continued at the mill until 1975 and various uses were found for different floors inside. The factory was converted to flats in 2004 and 2005.

Right: interior view of the mill in 1958. Originally the factory was lit by gas produced in the mill's own gasworks and the water for the steam boilers to power the machinery came from a reservoir fed by the Denton Holme millrace.

Denis Perriam

LINTON TWEEDS

WOOLLEN MANUFACTURERS
ESTABLISHED 1821.

ORNA · VERUM

Our registered Trade Mark is our guarantee of excellence.

LINTON'S CUMBERLAND HOMESPUNS, LTD.,
(formerly WADDELL'S. Ltd).,

CITADEL ROW,
CARLISLE.

In our warehouse stock on view, at Citadel Row, we have a very attractive range of men's suiting materials, in all weights and qualities.

We specially recommend our Cumberland Frieze at 17s. 6d. per yard, 56in. wide, for extra hard wear and especially suitable for working men's trousering.

We also hold a nice stock of Homespun material for sports suits at 12s. 6d. per yard, double width.

Come and see for yourselves, and if unable to call write us for patterns.

Special discount allowed to the trade.

Above: the shop at Linton Tweeds has a good range of fabric manufactured at the mill.
Right: advert for the mill from the early 1920s when their shop was on Citadel Row.

At Warwick Bridge the firm of William Waddell & Sons was well established but in 1912 the company was reformed as Waddell's Ltd under the joint directors, Cranston Waddell, William Linton and AG Greaves. Cranston Waddell died in 1917 and William Linton, as the sole surviving partner, renamed it Linton Cumberland Homespuns Ltd.

The move to Carlisle was made in 1919.

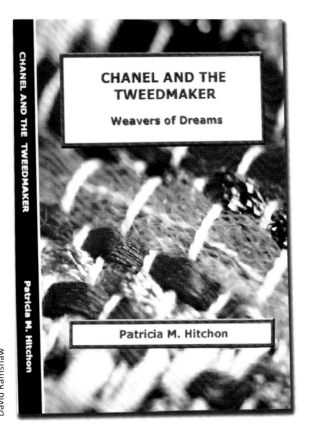

CHANEL AND THE TWEEDMAKER

CHANEL AND THE TWEEDMAKER

Weavers of Dreams

Patricia M. Hitchon

Patricia M. Hitchon

Left: the history of the firm is given fully in the book by Pat Hitchon.
Below: the relocation in 1919 was to the former weaving sheds of Dixon's Mill where the business is located today under the trading name of Linton Tweeds.

HOLME FOOT

Left: WH Nutter watercolour of Holme Foot House in 1869 with Caldew Bridge and Old Brewery in the distance. The flagpole stands on the River Caldew embankment.

Below left: 1865 OS map showing the position of the house on Milbourne Street.

Below: the University of Northumbria library built on the garden site in 2001.

There is nothing to indicate when Holme Foot was built, but a lease of 1774 refers to the millrace and on the east "was the ground and garden belonging to J Milbourne". The name Milbourne Street was given to the road leading through his land.

A Milbourne daughter married a Dixon and hence the Milbourne Dixons lived at Holme Foot House from the early 19th century and were still there in 1866 when the *Carlisle Journal* announced the death of George Thomas Dixon, "the third son of the late John Milbourne Dixon of Denton Holme, aged 45". The grander title of Denton Holme House was in use by 1860 but later reverted to its original name. When Denton Holme became a new suburb in 1852, Milbourne Dixon land was sold for housing and Holme Foot lost much of its tranquillity as a result.

When railway schemes were being discussed for the route of goods lines in 1872 mention was made in the *Carlisle Journal* of "Messrs Dixon's house at Holme Foot". But the family had left by 1875, because on the death of the last John Milbourne Dixon [there were three, grandfather, father and son] he was described as of Etterby Scaur.

Most of the garden at Holme Foot was destroyed when the Denton Holme Goods Yard was built in 1881.

For a short period in the 1880s this was the home of the Little Sisters of the Poor.

There were various later tenants but in September 1949 it was declared unfit for human habitation. The site was sold to Border Engineering and they used this as offices and storage yard. All was demolished for the erection of a new block of offices in 1960.

SEVEN WELLS

Above: the 1865 OS map shows Seven Wells Bank and an element of that was used as a street name in the Longsowerby estate.

Left: spring water still seeps out of the bottom of the river terrace just below St James Church in St James Park.

Above: the inscribed stone for St Lawrence's Well which formerly stood in the grounds of St James Church but is now inside.

Seven Wells Bank is a natural river terrace created by a meandering River Caldew. Beneath the bank were a series of springs which fed Spittal Crook a small stream.

In the medieval period, and possibly earlier, the pure water was venerated and it is thought there was a chapel where St James Church now stands, the field below having the name Chapel Field.

When plague threatened Carlisle in 1597 the sick were treated in isolation hospitals outside the city dependant on good supplies of fresh water. Wood was carried from Blackwell Wood by two wrights who spent two days "building the lodges at St Lawrence's Well". This temporary structure was soon abandoned but the hospital name stuck and the later Spittal Moor was chosen as the site of Carlisle Cemetery.

Right: behind these trees at the junction of Dalston Road and Richardson Street was Spittal House which took the name from the land farmed on Spittal Moor.

Denis Perriam all images

28

WELL FLATT

A flat was an open field without hedges, divided into strips. Different farmers rented strips which were widely dispersed - the idea being that farmers would get an equal share of good and bad land within a manor.

This system of farming died out in the middle ages. The well part of the name comes from the fact that the land was on Seven Wells Bank.

Land here belonged to the Priory of St Mary but at dissolution became the property of the Dean & Chapter of Carlisle Cathedral.

Let out as a small farm, Well Flatt stretched from Talbot Road to Longsowerby but as houses were built the farm retracted.

Denis Perriam all images

Top left: Well Flatt farmhouse on Dalston Road was built of clay with various extensions of brick all covered by render. This probably dated from the 17th century.

Top right: various families lived at Well Flatt over the years and the stone at Carlisle Cemetery commemorates Ralph Foster who died at Well Flatt on 7 November 1862. The sign came from the farm on demolition.

Above: the farm and associated buildings under demolition in 2004 for redevelopment.

Left: Well Flatt Cottage was built of whitewashed stone and stood on Dalston Road at the end of the walled farm orchard.

THOMAS NELSON

Left: Thomas Nelson's Marble Works next to Nelson Bridge. This was rail connected so stone could be brought in from Cove Quarry just over the Border for which Nelson had a lease. As well as his major contracting work building railways, fireplaces were carved here in marble for country houses and carved monuments for churches.

Plans to build the Victoria Viaduct meant the land was required so the marble works moved to Junction Street where it was connected to the Canal Branch. At this time, 1874, Thomas Nelson handed over the works to brother James.

The *Carlisle Patriot* states that Thomas Nelson "was born at Browhouses near Annan where his father was a contractor and worked some quarries". He was the son of Francis and Mary Nelson and was baptised at Gretna on 13 July 1807. The family moved to Dalston and it was there that his brother was born in 1821. Newspapers show that Thomas "came to Carlisle early in life and served his apprenticeship with Mr Sanderson". Having completed his apprenticeship he went to London where "he spent some time in an architect's office". This was for about two years because the *Carlisle Journal* states, "about the year 1830 he started business in Carlisle as a marble-mason".

At first he built himself a house on Lowther Street but by 1849 he had constructed Murrell Hill House. Thomas Nelson completed contracts all over the country as far away as Birmingham, Cardiff, Stranraer and Aberdeen. In retirement he went back to Dumfriesshire where he died in 1890.

Above: the small office building on Junction Street built in 1875 to serve the new marble works.

Above Right: Thomas Nelson lies next to his son JB Nelson at Carlisle Cemetery.

MURRELL HILL HOUSE

Sundour Shuttle

Left: Murrell Hill House was built for Thomas Nelson in the late 1840s.

Ashley Kendall

Denis Perriam

Left: the folly in the gardens of the house which was made from the clerestory windows of the Cathedral taken out by Thomas Nelson when he replaced these originals with replicas in the 1840s in a restoration of that part of the building.

Above: the Nelson Street lodge for the house which was demolished in 1937.

Below left: the 1860s marriage of Thomas Nelson's daughter Phina to Sir William Ferguson-Davie, the house forming the backdrop. Thomas left the house in 1872 for Friars Carse in Dumfriesshire, Murrell Hill being taken in 1876 by J Hewetson Brown. When he died it was again to let.

Below: trustees of Thomas Nelson offered Murrell Hill for sale in 1900 but it failed to reach its reserve and instead was let to Gavin Morton. He left in 1914 and it was bought by Morton Sundour to be used as an Auxiliary Hospital. In 1920 it converted to a recreation centre for Morton's workers. During World War Two it was used for housing troops and then by the ATS seen here. Demolition came in 1967.

Cumberland News

Sundour Shuttle

NELSON BRIDGE

Carlisle Library

Left: photograph taken in 1876 showing the bridge after it was raised in height for incorporation into the Victoria Viaduct. There is no picture of it prior to this date. The bridge determined the layout of Charlotte Street and Denton Street and was the only means of access to Denton Holme other than Caldew Bridge and a roundabout route.

Much detail is given on the bridge in the *Carlisle Journal* 25 June 1852. This was before it had a name and the newspaper suggested, "the new bridge should, out of compliment to the Mayor, be named 'Nelson Bridge'." Thomas Nelson had been the prime mover in the scheme and was to lay the foundation stone when he was Mayor, also contributing £500 of the costs. It was built by voluntary subscription totalling £3,400, the names given on an inscription on the parapet.

The bridge was to be completed in 1853 and the newspaper stated, "Denton Holme will by that time be studded with houses, as several streets have been projected, and some are already laid out." It was the bridge which made this possible and praise was given to Mr Nelson, "to his sagacity and foresight the town is mainly indebted, not merely for pointing out what ought to be done, but for showing how it could be done and for doing it in the right way at the right time."

It was estimated that from a former value of £150 per acre land in Denton Holme would increase to £2,160 an acre and therefore "the new bridge will have the effect of opening up a sort of 'gold diggins'".

Right: those who contributed towards the costs of the bridge are commemorated on a parapet inscription.

Mrs Dixon of Holme Foot gave £1,000
Messrs Ferguson Bros £650
John Ferguson & Co £500
Peter Dixon & Sons £200
Joseph Rome £200
The Corporation £200

They would all benefit from the construction.

THE NELSON BRIDGE.
THIS BRIDGE WAS BUILT BY THE FOLLOWING
SUBSCRIBERS AND COMPLETED A.D. 1853:
FAMILY OF THE LATE JOHN MILBOURNE DIXON,
FERGUSON BROTHERS, PETER DIXON & SONS,
JOHN FERGUSON & COMPANY,
JOSEPH ROME, THOMAS NELSON,
CORPORATION GAS WORKS COMMITTEE.

Denis Perriam

VICTORIA VIADUCT

VICTORIA VIADUCT
OPENED BY
HER ROYAL HIGHNESS THE PRINCESS LOUISE
20th SEPTEMBER 1877
COMMENCED 1876
JOSEPH BENDLE ESQUIRE, MAYOR
COMPLETED 1877
SAMUEL JACKSON BINNING ESQUIRE MAYOR

Above: the foundation stone in Shap Granite still to be seen on the Viaduct.

Above: the Victoria Viaduct looking over Nelson Bridge towards Denton Holme on the opening day with a triumphal arch.

Left: lamps based on the original design were replaced in 1997.

Below: the opening day with crowds watching Princess Louise cross the new viaduct. A specially constructed platform allowed the photographer from Annan & Co to take this view.

Integral to the construction of the Avoiding Goods Lines was a new viaduct to take traffic over them. This was a joint venture between the corporation and railway companies. Work began on the corporation portion on 18 November 1875, the contractor being Thomas Boustead Nelson. Robert Ward for the railway began on 15 November. There was demolition of property on Denton Crescent and Charlotte Street to raise the street level by 14 feet to a heightened Nelson Bridge. All was completed for an official opening by Princess Louise on 20 September 1877.

MILBOURNE STREET

There had been a road through Denton Holme from Caldew Bridge which ran parallel with the Denton Holme Millrace and passed Holme Foot where the Milbourne family lived. This served the various mills along the millrace and was the only access into Denton Holme from an early period.

As much of the land belonged to the Milbournes and was sold for housing development in the 1840s it was fitting that the new road with housing on each side should carry the Milbourne name.

This was the first development of terraced housing in Denton Holme which pre-dated Nelson Bridge. Land was for sale here in 1848 and an early reference is in the *Carlisle Journal* 17 December 1852 when "six newly erected houses on Milbourne Street" were for sale by David Little.

At first the properties built were back-to-back with courts behind. Overcrowding in the street was a problem and as early as 1857 John's Place behind Milbourne Street was described as "one of the dirtiest places in the town".

Where older housing did not conform to modern standards it was demolished in slum clearance, but Alan Harris stated "many of the back-to-back houses in this area were converted to 'through-houses' between 1938 and 1940". This saved them from demolition until the Ring Road threat.

Top: looking along the length of Milbourne Street from Richard Street in 1937.

Above: Graham's Court looking towards Milbourne Street, through the arch. Back-to-back housing like this had front doors facing into the court where the water came from a pump, shown in the centre, and around the walls of the court were closets and wash-houses used on a shared basis.

Right: view towards the mission hall and Holme Foot with Bridge Street in the distance.

Carlilsle Library two images

Denis Perriam

CHARLOTTE STREET

Above: the street sign now in Tullie House.

Left: houses in the street were, like Milbourne Street, back-to-back with courts behind.

Below: entrance arches led to the rear courtyards and many had distinctive diaper brickwork and individually carved keystones.

The *Carlisle Journal* 25 June 1852 gave an outline of what was proposed once Nelson Bridge was completed. "from the end of the bridge another street will lead off almost at right angles…. by this street there will be direct communication between the canal and the railway and a great deal of heavy traffic that now passes through the principal streets of the town will be advantageously diverted".

Because the land belonged to the Milbourne Dixon family and this was the year of the marriage of Charlotte Milbourne Dixon to Thomas Sheffield, the new street was given her name.

Houses were still being built here in 1863 the *Carlisle Journal* advertising "six newly-erected and tenanted dwelling houses with w/cs and palisading in front. Also twelve in the same street in the course of erecting by James Briggs joiner and builder".

Most of the houses were later modernised and the main reason for demolition in 1976 was to make way for the Ring Road.

Previously houses had come down in 1881 to make way for a railway extension.

Left: the street curved to join with Milbourne Street and also straight on to join Junction Street.

DENTON HOLME ESTATE

Denis Perriam

Left: housing erected on Society plots in Cumberland Street in the 1850s.

Below: book giving the aims and history of the Cumberland Building Society.

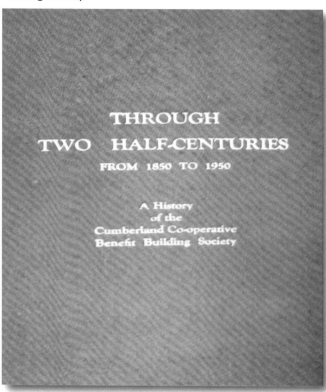

On the formation of the Cumberland Cooperative Benefit Building Society in 1851 a resolution was passed to "support the industrial classes of Carlisle". The object was to "purchase land…. and apportion it to allotments suitable for building…. at the price it cost the Society". This could be done by members paying as little as 6d per week for a plot which would cost £25. Land was purchased by the Society from Joseph Rome in 1852 and "the ground was assigned by ballot to 71 members…. and by the end of 1854 a considerable number of houses had been erected in Westmorland, Cumberland and Dale Streets as part of the project".

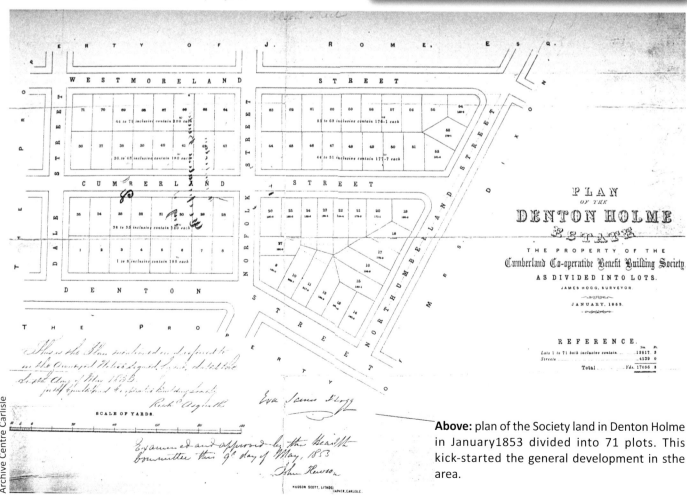

Archive Centre Carlisle

Above: plan of the Society land in Denton Holme in January1853 divided into 71 plots. This kick-started the general development in sthe area.

STREETS

CONSTABLE ST

William Constable was works manager at Holme Head Works and a former master at Holme Head School..

RICHARDSON ST.

The Richardson family owned land between Norfolk Street and the Cemetery.

LORNE CRESCENT

Queen Victoria's daughter married the Marquis of Lorne in 1871 and there was national celebration for this event.

NELSON St.

This is named after Thomas Nelson who had a large house on the street and laid it out. Some of these original blue enamel signs are to be found in Denton Holme but this one has now gone.

FREER STREET

Freer and Blunt was the firm of solicitors who dealt with the sale of the Denton Holme estate. As the firm was based in Leicester there is also Leicester Street but it never had a sign.

Above: the finishing touches being put to Freer Street in the 1930s with the tarmac being laid.

METCALFE STREET

Carlisle Library

Above: Metcalfe Street was built by Robert Metcalfe.

ASHMAN CLOSE

Alan Ashman, manager of Carlisle United took the club into the first division in 1974. Streets in this development off Richardson Street have a local football theme.

TRAFALGAR ST

In the mistaken belief that Nelson Street was named after the admiral, Trafalgar Street and Collingwood Street were so named, Admiral Collingwood taking charge at Trafalgar with the death of Nelson.

SHEFFIELD St

John Sheffield married Elizabeth Milbourne Dixon on 20 July 1852 and as this street was laid out at that time and the land belonged to Margaret's family it was given this name.

RANDALL St.

Street signs: Findlay Stirling & Denis Perriam

John Milbourne Dixon married Charlotte Randall in 1815 and this resulted in the names Charlotte Street and Randall Street.

ST JAMES CHURCH

Denis Perriam three images

Left: the church on its hilltop setting.

Right: bizarrely the church and vicar appeared on cigarette cards and the date would be between 1919 and 1933 when the Rev Hopkins was the incumbent. The same photograph appears on a calendar for 1926.

Rev. F. W. Hopkins, M.A.

Carlisle Library

The need for a Church of England church to serve an ever increasing population in Denton Holme was answered by the creation of a new parish in 1861. Worship was held at first in Holme Head School.

A plot was secured in an elevated position overlooking the parish and building work began in 1865 to the designs of Anderson & Pepper of Bradford at a total cost of £4,500. Prime mover in the scheme was the Countess of Waldegrave, a relative of the Bishop, she laying the foundation stone and attending the opening ceremony on 25 July 1867, St James Day.

Above: the marriage at the church on 12 August 1967 of Jean Perriam and Frank Eastwood. Jean had been a member of the church YPF.

Chulrch Centenary Booklet

Above: the church interior. At the east end is a stained glass window commemorating members of the Nelson family.

Below: the church foundation stone laid on 12 September 1865.

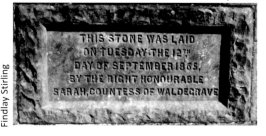

Findlay Stirling

THIS STONE WAS LAID
ON TUESDAY THE 12TH
DAY OF SEPTEMBER 1865,
BY THE RIGHT HONOURABLE
SARAH, COUNTESS OF WALDEGRAVE

Above: the vicarage on Dalston Road was just outside the parish and was built before the church thanks to a generous grant from the Ecclesiastical Commissioners. Here it is seen when converted to the Caldew Hospital and it faces demolition in 2018.

ST JAMES SCHOOL

Left: St James School designs by James Nelson dated 29 March 1872.

Below: the Bishop of Carlisle lays the foundation stone in 1993 for the extensions.

When the original idea for this building was promoted in December 1870 the *Carlisle Journal* stated it was to have a two-fold purpose as a Sunday School and for infants during the week. It was to cost £500. But schools inspector Claude Parez thought a year later it should "be purely a girls' school". This was built as St James National School to serve Cummersdale and St James parish in 1872 and was known locally as the High School. With the creation of a school board and the building of Morley Street School and another planned at Cummersdale this was made redundant in 1877 as a public elementary school and remained in possession of the church. Closure had been because of its "position and discomforts". It had served various purposes when a school - being used as a meeting room, a Sunday school and for adult cookery classes. Extensions were planned in 1971.

The Mission Hall on Blencowe Street had been the main parish hall but with modernisation needed it was decided to sell that site and extend the former school instead for use as a parish centre.

Above: as it is today.

Left: the architect's designs for the extensions which were completed for opening in 1993. The vicar stated "our overall aim is to provide a composite building with facilities for all ages, to serve the community in the parish of Denton Holme from a Christian perspective".

MISSION HALLS

Left: the Blencowe Mission Hall during demolition in 1990 to be replaced by flats. A new Church Centre in the former school next to the church and the Cornerstone facility replaced this.

Below: the designs for the Mission Hall in 1882 by J Murchie.

With further housing in Denton Holme in the 1870s there was a need for additional church accommodation for Sunday schools and a hall for meetings. This resulted in the construction of the Mission Hall on Blencowe Street which opened in 1883. This still did not meet the needs of a parish spread over a wide area and another mission was built on Milbourne Street.

Below: the 1900 OS map showing the corner location of the Blencowe Street Mission Hall.

Below left: the 1894 corrugated-iron mission on Milbourne Street. This was built to accommodate 250 people and had previously been in a building in Slack's Court which had become too small for those attending.

Below: procession about to set off from the Milbourne Street hall in the 1920s.

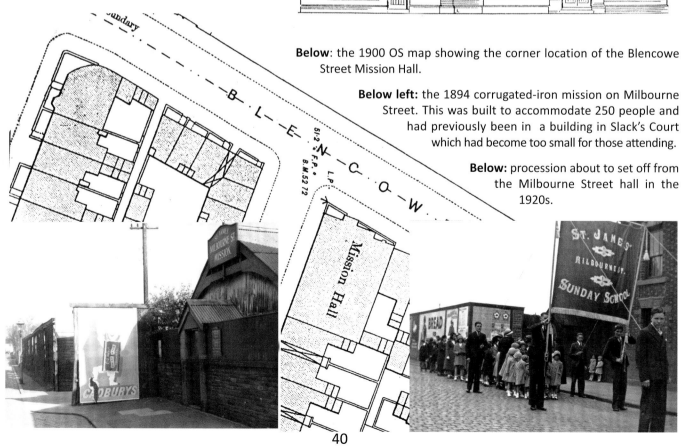

CONGREGATIONAL CHURCH

Denis Perriam

Above: the foundation stone laid 30 April 1860. Built to the designs of John Crossley at a cost of over £5,000.

Left: the church on its island site. The building was cleaned with a government grant in 1973.

A group of Congregationalists broke away from the Lowther Street church and after meeting in the Mechanics' Institute bought land in Charlotte Street to build a church of their own. It opened for worship on 3 May 1861. With an increasing number of worshippers it was necessary to install a gallery in 1867. There was still not enough room and extensions were carried out in 1878 for a Sunday School, Institute and Lecture Hall. The church amalgamated with the United Reform Church in 1972 and the congregation moved to Warwick Road. This was then used by the Jehovah Witness organisation and today it is used as a church by the Carlisle Christian Fellowship.

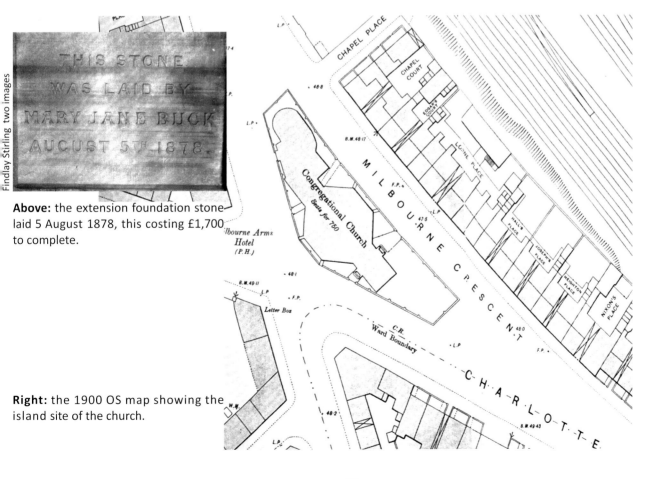

Findlay Stirling two images

Above: the extension foundation stone laid 5 August 1878, this costing £1,700 to complete.

Right: the 1900 OS map showing the island site of the church.

ATLAS HALL

Left: plans for an office block for Pratchitts were submitted in July 1965 and this photograph in 1966 shows the Atlas Hall being demolished to make way for the new building. This is the only known view of the building.

Below: the 1900 OS map showing the site on the corner of Denton Street and Lorne Street.

Plans for the Denton Street Christian Mission House were submitted to the city council in 1872. Previously this group of Christians had met in what was originally the Methodist Chapel on Fisher Street which became the site of the Richmond Hall. Details of the opening service in Denton Holme were given in the *Carlisle Express* in November 1872 with a similar report in the *Carlisle Journal*.

As the 'Church of Christ', the Denton Street chapel was advertised in the *North Cumberland Reformer* in December 1893. This was in advance of this sect building a new church on the corner of Grey Street and Edward Street, the later Elim Church. The opening of this new church was reported in the *Carlisle Journal* in June 1894. While the Denton Street chapel is mentioned in a 1901 directory it does not say what it was used for at the time. But an editorial in the *Carlisle Journal* for May 1912 explains that Messrs RR Buck and Sons had extended, both at Nelson Street "and the old chapel at the corner of Lorne Street.... turned by the firm to industrial uses".

The newspaper again referred to the chapel in October 1921 when it reported that it had not been used for religious purposes for about 10 years and during the war was a parcel packing depot for the Citizens' League.

It was "to be converted into a recreational hall for Atlas Works by Messrs Buck" and was to be called 'Atlas Hall'.

City minutes for 1939 show that the licence for music and dancing for the hall was not renewed. In the 'Local Chatter' column of the *Carlisle Journal* in May 1939 it stated that the hall had "been acquired by the Unitarian body". They met for their last service in Blackfriars Street in June, the newspaper reporting that they were "moving to the Atlas Hall", where their new chapel was dedicated in the autumn.

When the Unitarians ceased to meet there in 1956 the city was anxious to purchase it as a possible community centre, but at a cost of £4,000 to convert, this did not happen. Instead city minutes for March 1957 show a change of use from church hall to workshop for the manufacture of woodcraft articles for G Gillieran; then in March 1958 a further change from workshop to warehouse for Eden Wholesale Suppliers.

Extensions for that use were approved in minutes for 1958-59.

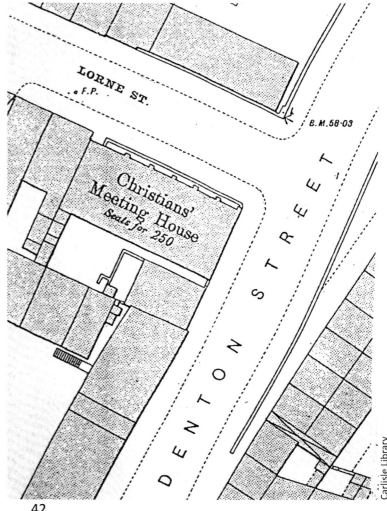

GRAHAM STREET METHODISTS

A Primitive Methodist school-church was planned for Graham Street in 1881. This was ambitious as the build costs were £560 and only £230 had been raised by subscription. So a school was built first and as the funds were never forthcoming the church was not built. Instead the school served as a church and Sunday School. This eventually became redundant and in 1943 it became an Elim Church.

Later it became a plumber's workshop until demolition to make way for flats.

Above: the school building adapted as the chapel in later use as a plumber's workshop with alterations.

Below: the *Carlisle Journal* 9 August 1881 report of the Carlisle Urban Sanitary Authority made it seem the entire plan had been carried out.

The New Primitive Methodist Chapel.—A letter was read from the Rev. W. Saul, on behalf of the trustees of the Primitive Methodist Chapel and Sunday School in Graham Street, Denton Holme, stating that the building was about completed, that the Urban Sanitary Authority were liable to flag, channel, and pave in front of the building, and the trustees would be obliged if the Committee would order the work to be done with the least possible delay.—The Surveyor: It is not a complete street.—The Town Clerk said the Authority had done nothing at the street yet by which they could recover money. If they did expend money they could not recover their proportion from the trustees or incumbent of a place of worship in actual existence when the work was done, but they were not bound to spend any money on the street.—Mr. Milburn: But he is willing to pay. (Laughter.)—The Town Clerk: No, he wants the Urban Authority to do it at the expense of the rates.—The Chairman: I suppose he is his own lawyer.—It was agreed that the Town Clerk should reply to the letter in accordance with the tenour of his remarks.

Above: the 1900 OS map showing the school as the chapel.

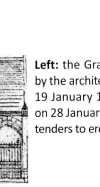

Left: the Graham Street façade as planned by the architect Joseph Shields of Durham on 19 January 1881. While this was approved on 28 January the church was never built yet tenders to erect were invited on 22 February.

43

HOLME HEAD BRITISH SCHOOL

Ferguson Centenary Book

Above: detail of a lithograph of Ferguson Bros factory in 1850s showing the school on the left-hand side.

The school was established in the early 1840s by Joseph Ferguson "for the education of the children of the operatives" at the Holme Head factory. One of the pupils who had entered the school on 30 July 1866 was James Lattimer and he reminisced; "the desks were ranged along one side of this large room, without divisions of any kind, with the master's desk and a stove beside the opposite wall, from which the master could survey all his pupils at a glance. The master looked towards the adjoining works while the pupils faced the cemetery." By the time James Lattimer entered the school had been enlarged "by the addition of a classroom and sewing room with cloakrooms in between". He stated that "the floor of the classroom was built in steps, high enough for the children to sit on, which they approached by smaller steps at the side, arranged two walking steps to each sitting step". Here the lowest two classes were taught to read, write and to do sums on frameless slates with slate pencils.

This was the only school in Denton Holme until the building of St James School in 1872. When inspected in 1871 Holme Head had 300 pupils but with the opening of Morley Street School in 1884 the Holme Head one closed. Annual reunions of old pupils were held until the early 1950s when with dwindling numbers these ceased.

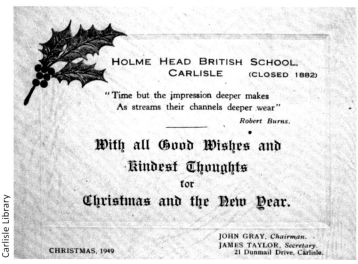

Carlisle Library

Above: the Christmas card sent to each member of the association, the last one sent in 1951.

Jean Atkinson

Right: cup presented to the oldest member of the old scholars association who attended the annual reunions. This was won in 1944 by Joseph McGregor who was then 87.

FOOTBRIDGES

Denis Perriam, two images

Left: the 1885 Holme Head footbridge.

Below: the South Vale Bridge of 1925.

A bridge over the Caldew in Denton Holme had long been under discussion but the council were reluctant to meet the expense. Instead Joseph Ferguson agreed to erect a footbridge at a cost of £300 at Holme Head. This was a suspension bridge constructed by Messrs Burgess, Robson & Armstrong to designs by John Hodgson. Structural problems led to this being replaced in 1885.

There were stepping stones linking East Dale Street to Rome Street and it was hoped by some that a road bridge would be built there. A fatality there in 1909 made the scheme more urgent but the war intervened. A proposal for a footbridge was made in 1922. After delays this opened in 1925. With flood defence work in 2008 a replacement high level footbridge was installed in 2010.

Brian Irwin

Findlay Stirling

This bridge was re-named
Nicholson Bridge
on 25 June 2010
in memory of Kim Nicholson
Environment Agency Area Manager
2002-2007

Above: the 2010 replacement Nicholson footbridge at East Dale Street.

Left: the plaque on the 2010 bridge giving the new name.

ROBERT FERGUSON SCHOOL

Mary Eite, two images

Left: a 1920s view of the school from Dale Street showing the caretaker's house on the left and the distinctive boiler house chimney.

Houses are yet to be built on the opposite side of Denton Street which makes this viewpoint impossible today.

Below: miniature portrait of Robert Ferguson as a young man by Thomas Heathfield Carrick.

Land had been purchased here in advance by the Carlisle School Board and the Education Act of 1902 gave sanction to build a new school to be known as the Robert Ferguson Board School. Ferguson had done much to encourage education in Carlisle and this was a fitting tribute to his memory.

Designs were prepared by Walter H Brierly of York to accommodate 360 senior mixed pupils and 360 infants in 1902 and this was put out to tender in November. The chosen contractors were Messrs J&R Bell at a cost of £8,977 2s 8d. Work was completed for an opening in September 1904.

There were still some additions and in March 1905 tenders were invited for the caretaker's house and boundary wall.

John Ferguson

Above: at about the same time boys are seen in the spacious playground, girls and infants probably occupy the adjoining playground. As well as these spaces there were playing fields in grassland beyond.

ROBERT FERGUSON SCHOOL

Above: Walter Eite was the headmaster and remained so until his retirement.

Above: pupils, teachers and possibly some parents are seen posed against the school wall dressed in costume when taking part in the 1928 Carlisle Pageant.

Right: the infant class at the school in 1955.

ROBERT FERGUSON INFANTS' SCHOOL, CARLISLE, 1955

Above: with lack of room in the existing school for ever increasing numbers of secondary pupils, four huts were added in a corner of the playing field in 1958. Here is a 1961 group outside one of the huts.

Right: first issue of the school magazine in 1963 featuring the school badge. Only three issues were published before closure.

Left: with the introduction of comprehensive education Robert Ferguson closed as a Secondary Modern. The infants remained and juniors at Morley Street were transferred to Robert Ferguson. A suitably-named minibus takes pupils on school outings.

47

MORLEY STREET SCHOOL

Above: the former Boys School at the corner of Morley Street and Northumberland Street became a part of Robert Fergusons - classrooms being used for Chemistry and Art lessons. Metalwork and Woodwork were taught in low-level buildings along Westmorland Street.

The street was named after Edward Taylor Morley, who died in December 1876. As City Surveyor he had done much in the street layout of Denton Holme. Denton Holme Board School, to include infants, boys and girls, was planned by Daniel Birkett in 1879 to the same designs as Caldewgate School. The contract went to C&J Armstrong using their own Kingstown machine made bricks with white stone dressings from Howrigg Quarry.

Carlisle library two images

Above: part of the former school is now used as a community centre where Neighbourhood Forum meetings and other events are held. It also houses a branch library.

The school opened in November 1880 at a cost of £7,500 with a caretaker's house costing an additional £400. There were extensions in 1885 and again in 1894. Figures for average attendance in 1900 were 347 boys, 341 girls and 427 infants. There were changes when Robert Ferguson School opened. Two rooms were set aside at Morley Street for 20 Delicate Children in 1908 and when inspected in 1909 was approved "and attracted a good deal of interest".

George Winter became the headmaster in 1953 and retired in 1968. Part of the school was then used by Robert Ferguson School and in Autumn 1970 all pupils were transferred to Robert Fergusons as part of the reorganisation of secondary education. Plans were then put in hand to find new uses for the school.

Denis Perriam

Left: the junior class of 1956 overseen by teacher Miss Fisher posed in the playground.

AIDANVISION

Evening News and Star

Left: pupils at work in the studio.

Right: publicity leaflet giving technical details.

Cumberland News

Above: pupils with one of the cameras in 1976.

In *Arts North* in March 1979, Roy Thompson explained, "Aidanvision started at St Aidan's School in 1972 when Border Television converted to colour and the school's art department purchased all video monochrome equipment". This he said was an "innovative move which sought to serve educational needs within the large co-educational school and to provide 'open door' facilities for other video users".

The move to Denton Holme came, stated Mr Thompson, "as the equipment fast outgrew the available space at the school. Northern Arts commissioned a plausibility study to explore the needs of such an operation and shortly afterwards a near perfect site, a large disused school in Morley Street was offered to Aidanvision rent and rates free".
A publicity leaflet explained that the facility was available to local businesses by subscription as members. This it was hoped would "bring to industrialists the use of the communications medium at a professional standard and at a price which will not deter businessmen from using the most important information medium ever invented".
On offer were "make-up and changing rooms, a general workshop fitted for the manufacture of sets and scenery and adequate provision for the storage of properties". There was also seminar and production rooms available to visiting producers and directors. The *Cumberland News* 25 November 1988 reported on a new headquarters for Cumbria's Pocket Theatre; "the group is to lease the former Aidanvision Studio from Cumbria County Council". The report continued, "Aidanvision Studios building is used occasionally by Carlisle area schools using video recording equipment funded by Northern Arts, the British Film Institute and St Aidan's School and Pocket Theatre is to continue to develop this use".

The three-year lease was not renewed and demolition came in 1991.

Bottom: when businesses were invited to use the studio membership details were given in this leaflet.

Denis Perriam, two images

49

CANAL BRANCH RAILWAY

Left: the Canal Branch passing through Murrell Hill and Denton Holme soon after opening. This was included in JW Carmichael's *Views on the Newcastle & Carlisle Railway* published in 1839 but was based on drawings he had done while the railway was under construction in 1835.

Below: there was an original cattle-creep where Blencowe Street was later laid out and the sandstone bridge remained until 1973.

It was intended that a goods only branch would extend the Newcastle & Carlisle Railway from London Road Station to the Canal Basin and work began on this in 1834 ready for opening in 1837. This required a number of bridges and a large embankment, the contractor being George Grahamsley.

At first this brought coal and lime from the Brampton collieries to Carlisle and for export along the canal. This part of the line opened before that to Newcastle.

A stone bridge over the Caldew had been built by Grahamsley but it collapsed in 1846 and had to be replaced by a temporary wooden structure and then by successive girder bridges. With gradual removal of sections of embankment since closure in 1969 there is little to show that the railway existed.

Above: a girder bridge replaced the 'Red Arch' on Denton Street in 1852. This was widened with this bridge in 1900 to make way for trams. It remained until 1974.

Left: an embankment carried the railway across Denton Holme an idea of the height is given in this view when part of the earthworks was removed to widen Blencowe Street in 1993. The stone from the bridge abutment was used in the restoration of the Cathedral.

Denis Perriam, all images

DALSTON ROAD CROSSING

The Canal Branch opened 9 March 1837 with a level crossing at Murrell Hill as it was then known. There was no signal box then and the gates would have to be opened manually by a crossing keeper, who would have been kept busy as this was the main road route into Denton Holme. Protection for the gate keeper was provided by a stone booth which was eventually superseded by the signal box.

Closure came on 3 August 1969 and the gates were permanently open until the track was lifted in 1970. The signal box was soon demolished along with the booth but that was re-erected in a garden at Corby Hill.

All traces of the crossing were removed with road improvements in the 1970s.

Above: John Johnston seen at the signal box in the 1940s where he worked for many years before retiring in 1959.

Top: the level crossing looking east in the 1960s.

Top right: the stone crossing-keeper's booth.

Bottom right: the 1837 crossing-keeper's house adjoining the signal box.

AVOIDING GOODS LINES

Left: work in progress in 1877 on the bridge over the Caldew which carried the Avoiding Goods Lines into Denton Holme. In the background can be seen Nelson Bridge with the gas works beyond. Construction work on the approaches to Nelson Bridge for the Victoria Viaduct can be seen along with buildings on the right in Brocklebank's timber yard.

Below left: the crash on 1 May 1984 which damaged the above bridge and permanently closed the goods lines.

With the proposed Settle & Carlisle line plans were made to cope with the increased freight traffic into the city. It was decided to separate goods and passenger trains so that freight would bypass the station and instead new lines would carry goods over the Caldew through Denton Holme.

Land was acquired in 1874 and construction work began in 1875 for completion in 1877. Plans for opening the new line were made in July 1877 but there was a delay.

Left: with the goods lines closed and no prospect of them ever reopening the remaining lines under the viaduct were lifted in 1987.

Right: it was decided to use the former railway as a riverside footpath and cycleway and this was opened in 1996. There were plans to reopen the line in 1999 but these came to nothing.

DENTON HOLME GOODS DEPOT

Left: a new joint goods depot was to be built in Denton Holme traffic coming in from the Avoiding Goods Lines. Tenders were invited in September 1880 for a goods shed and office building with a goods yard behind Milbourne Street. All was completed for use in 1882.

Above: deliveries were made from the depot around the streets by horse-drawn lorries and when the transition was made to motors in the 1950s the Scammel replacements were called mechanical horses. Here in 1954 is a group of award winning drivers.

Above and below: when the Avoiding Goods Lines closed in 1984 the goods shed was still rail connected. With the decision made to close the railway the connecting railway bridge over the Caldew into the yard was demolished in 1987.

Left: Robert Forrester's atmospheric oil of the goods yard in 1962.

TRAMS

Denis Perriam

Tullie House Museum and Art Gallery Trust

Above: on 29 June 1900 there was a test run of the trams into Denton Holme and the first one stuck under the railway bridge. This seems to be that occasion because it is otherwise an unusual place to stop the tram and gather such a crowd.

Above right: enclosed tramcar No 2 on Denton Street near the terminus at Holme Head. Robert Ferguson school is visible on the left in this view of 1907.

A single track electric tramway with passing places ran over the viaduct and for the full length of Denton Street. Trams ran every 10 minutes at peak times from 30 June 1900 until 21 November 1931. Because of the bridge clearance of 12ft 11 inches single-deckers were used. The first fleet of chocolate-brown and cream livery was replaced in 1912 by new vehicles which were dark green and cream lined out in cream and red. Single fares were one penny and from 1912 there was a through service to London Road.

There were accidents and in February 1903 three boys ran in front of a tram when it was in motion. The driver cut off the power and applied the emergency brake but the tram hit the last boy who had both legs severed. He died in the infirmary soon afterwards.

Ashley Kendall

Left: a tramcar caught up in a Denton Street procession in the 1920s.

BUS SERVICES

Two motor buses, Pussyfoot and Tishy, were used on the route to Longsowerby in 1923. With no prospect of the tram service being extended to new housing estates operators took advantage of this anomaly. But even where trams were available on the Holme Head route there was bus competition by 1924.

As well as Campbell operating a bus from Harraby to Holme Head in 1924 there was a service offered by George Little from the Town Hall to Holme Head. In the same year John Parker and Robert Henry Thomlinson ran a bus from the Town Hall to Longsowerby. Fred Hart ran a service through Denton Holme to Cummersdale.

Above: the annual bus inspection in July 1926 showing the Holme Head one in Market Street. This vehicle was registered to Roderick Clerc Campbell, 30 Portland Place.

Above: the 665 Ribble service to Holme Head seen here in the late 1960s in Rickergate. The service ran to Kingstown so this was on a return journey.

Above: the first Ribble double-decker bus into Denton Holme in April 1954 while the road beneath the railway bridge over Denton Street was being lowered. John Huggon with his bicycle is one of the boys

Bus operator Sydney P Adair was living in Westmorland Street when he was prosecuted for carrying 26 passengers in a 14-seater bus. The Adair brothers ran a works service from Raffles to Richardson Street for Holme Head workers.

On 31 August 1931 bus services in Carlisle were taken over by Ribble and they ran a single-decker service through Denton Holme which was much in demand after the withdrawal of trams on 21 November that year.

Between 1934 and 1939 Ribble ran a service along Charlotte Street to Wigton Road.

With road improvements double-decker buses could be used from 1954 along Denton Street. Stagecoach now operate the city centre buses but Reays also run a bus service through Denton Holme.

Below: 69 Stagecoach bus at Holme Head terminus in June 2018 about to set off for Edentown.

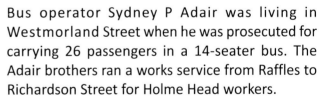

MURRELL HILL BRICKS

Denis Perriam, two images

Because of the geological make-up of Murrell Hill there were good deposits of clay which were ideal for brick making. Bricks were not manufactured in quantity in Carlisle until the late 17th century. When Matthew Wilman, a bricklayer, died in 1684 an inventory of his possessions included £10 "for half of the Murrell Hill Brick Kiln".

Bricks have been made there at different periods but it was not until 1854, under the ownership of Thomas Nelson, that a brickworks was constructed there. This was beside the Canal Branch and a siding helped in transporting finished bricks. In the 1870s Nelson converted the buildings to a sawmill and on 1 July 1891 this was let to Thomas Niven who eventually purchased. That firm continued to trade until 2001.

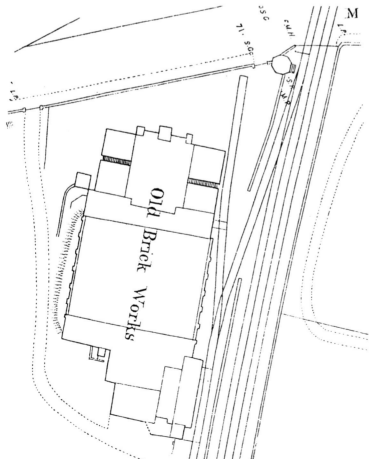

Carlisle Library

Above left: the former brickworks in use by Thomas Niven.

Above right: the closure notice from the *Cumberland News*.

Left: the buildings shown on the 1900 OS map.

Below: clearing the site for the Cumbrian Newspapers car park.

CUMBERLAND NEWS

Denis Perriam, two images

Left: the 1971 *Cumberland News* offices on Dalston Road now having the title of Cumbrian Newspapers.

Below: Princess Anne accompanied by John Burgess leaving the building after the opening ceremony.

The *Carlisle Patriot* was first published on 3 June 1815. This newspaper was merged with the *East Cumberland News* to form the *Cumberland News* in 1910, a weekly issue.

The association with the Burgess family came when John Burgess joined the company in 1867 to become editor in 1868.

Cumberland News

It was his son, Robert Nelson Burgess, who created the *Cumberland News.*

The newspaper office had been on English Street with the printing press behind in Lowthian's Lane and this was rebuilt in 1925. These premises became outdated and with no room for expansion the decision was taken to build instead at Murrell Hill in 1970. Extensions were made with new printing facilities in 2013. With the impact of social media on newspaper sales it was decided by the board and chairman Robin Burgess to sell the CN Group to Newsquest Media in 2018.

To commemorate the visit of
THE PRINCESS ROYAL
22nd July 2015
to mark the 200th Anniversary of
THE CUMBERLAND NEWS
1815 - 2015

Barry Beckett

THE STONE WAS LAID BY
SIR MAURICE LAING
ON 3rd MAY 1971

Above: Princess Anne returned in 2015 marking the bicentenary of the paper.

Above : Sir Maurice Laing laid this commemorative stone in 1971.

LAING

Above: an advert for the firm when the yard was on Milbourne Street. During World War One they relocated to Dalston Road.

Top left: John Laing built Sebergham Terrace on St James Road in 1882 using cream bricks and lived in No 42. This was later the home of JW Laing.

In the early 19th century David Laing established a construction business at Sebergham and his son James followed his father as a builder. It was John Laing, James' eldest son, who brought the business in 1874 to Carlisle plans being approved in 1878 for an office and store on Newcastle Street.

The building yard was on Milbourne Street and their first large contract was the Little & Ballantyne building on the Victoria Viaduct in 1882.

Reminiscing about the firm, Stanley Laing stated that he started to work for them in 1912. At that time "they just had a small wooden office and yard on Milbourne Street". It was John William Laing, son of John, born in Carlisle in 1879 who was to develop the firm into a world-wide enterprise. Stanley Laing stated, "John Laing was always going round the sites on a bicycle with a little auto wheel like an autocycle. Many a time he left his bike and didn't know where he had left it".

The company was sold in 2001 to O'Rourke Construction to become Laing O'Rourke.

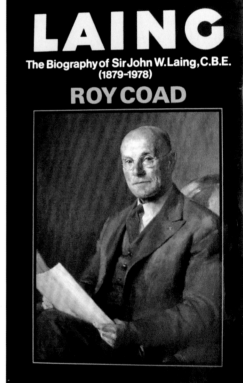

LAING

The Biography of Sir John W. Laing, C.B.E. (1879-1978)

ROY COAD

Carlisle Library

Above: much has been written about the history of the firm; this book and *The Good Builder* by Berry Ritchie.

Denis Perriam two images

Left: the original Laing's yard was on this site on Milbourne Street next to the former Woolpack Inn.

J & R BELL

— FRONT ELEVATION —

Left: 47 Nelson Street built by Robinson Bell as his own house to the designs of John Hodgson, the plans approved 1 October 1897.

Bottom left: members of the Bell family outside their original house in Sheffield Street.

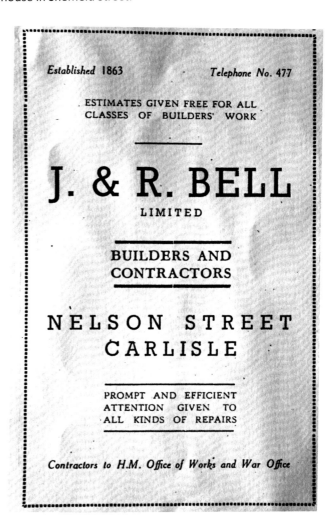

Established 1863 · Telephone No. 477

ESTIMATES GIVEN FREE FOR ALL CLASSES OF BUILDERS' WORK

J. & R. BELL
LIMITED

BUILDERS AND CONTRACTORS

NELSON STREET CARLISLE

PROMPT AND EFFICIENT ATTENTION GIVEN TO ALL KINDS OF REPAIRS

Contractors to H.M. Office of Works and War Office

Carlisle Directory 1938

At one time J&R Bell were more important in the construction industry than Laing, being the main contractor for various government departments. Many Denton Holme buildings were constructed by the firm, choosing to have a yard on Nelson Street in 1897. Founded in 1863 the company secured many local contracts which included the conversion of public houses for the Central Control Board. They built the Alma Block in Carlisle Castle, the Employment Exchange in Rickergate, the Telephone Repeater Station at Harraby, pithead baths at St Helen's Colliery at Siddick and the Milk Marketing Board's Creamery at Aspatria. As well as restoration work on Carlisle Cathedral they extended the Cumberland Infirmary and Public Baths; built the bus stations, Lakeland Laundry and a number of churches and parish halls.

In both wars they were fully involved in war contracts. About 1949 the firm ceased business.

Plans were submitted in October 1950 for the conversion of 47 into two flats for the Bell family. By March 1954 Robert Liddle had the building and he had his yard behind. He died in 1964 and Border Plant Hire took

over his business. Seymour Plant Ltd converted 47 into two flats once again. City Minutes in 1972 show that the property was conveyed by Seymour to the Corporation for the Water Department. This was then leased by the NWWA for 15 years from 1 April 1974. With the move of NW Water in 1998, 47 was for sale in January 1998 becoming the offices for a Housing Association. Since then it has been converted to flats.

The large workshop behind 47 was converted to Centre 47 with extensions for offices of Impact Housing Association.

VICTORIA FOUNDRY

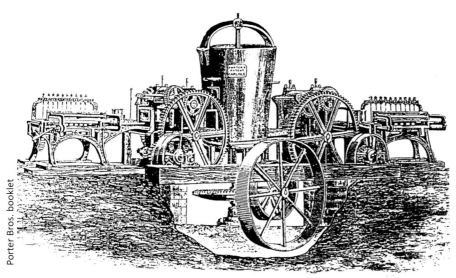

Porter Bros. booklet

Above: still to be found in Carlisle are Porter's products.
Left: a Porter's patent double brick-making machine. They also made mill machinery as well as simple castings.

Messrs George Graham of the Victoria Foundry on Denton Street advertised in the *Carlisle Journal* 30 May 1879 that as an iron and brass founder they made manhole covers and lamp poles. The firm again advertised in September 1881 that they manufactured gully traps under Clark's patent and the Denton Street works were for sale as they were erecting another foundry at Maryport. In October the newspaper reported on Graham's bankruptcy [he died in Manchester in 1891 aged 68].

The Victoria Foundry was acquired by the newly formed [but old established] Porter Brothers in 1882 who moved from Blackfriars Street. With a name change to Porter Engineering they continued on this site until 1998 when the business was dissolved.

Below left: as the company modernised new offices were opened on the Denton Street and Collingwood Street corner.

Below right: advert from 1967 when the company future seemed assured.

End Outlet Gully, with Sludge Basket complete.

Sizes—10in. x 7in., 12in. x 8in., 14in. x 10in.,

Denis Perriam

Above: one of Clark's patent gully traps which were cast by Graham and also by Porters.

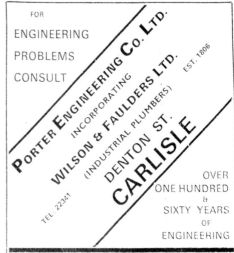

FOR ENGINEERING PROBLEMS CONSULT

PORTER ENGINEERING Co. LTD.
INCORPORATING
WILSON & FAULDERS LTD.
(INDUSTRIAL PLUMBERS)
EST. 1806
DENTON ST.
CARLISLE
TEL. 22341

OVER ONE HUNDRED & SIXTY YEARS OF ENGINEERING

Carlisle Guide 1967

DENTON IRON WORKS

Denis Perriam

Above left: inside the works in 1959.
Below left: booklet produced to celebrate 100 years of Pratchitts.

Above right: the company gate clock in 1958.

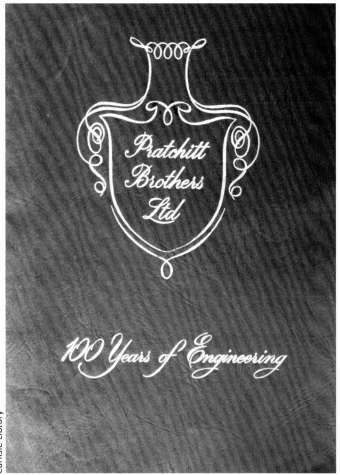

Carlisle Library

The firm of Blaylock and Pratchitt was formed in 1859 producing ticket dating presses for railways under Edmundson's patent at Long Island Works. As the company expanded a site was purchased in Denton Holme on 4 February 1863, work on the erection of Denton Iron Works starting immediately. Fixed and portable steam engines were their speciality but all kinds of pumping machinery was manufactured. Early contracts included ironwork for railway stations on the CKPR and NBR from Carlisle to Langholm. As Pratchitt Brothers the firm received a Royal Warrant from Edward VII for pumping installations at Sandringham in 1904. Later the firm was known for its industrial dryers and was taken over by LA Mitchell. New offices were erected in 1967. The works closed in 2016.

Below right: founding partner in the firm, William Pratchitt, born in 1833.

Below left: a rotary calciner weighing 24 tons in transit from the works.

Pratchitt's Centenary booklet, three images

61

WHITFIELD & HOWE

Denis Perriam, two images

Left: Lorne Street with Lorne Works just beyond the car and the chimney behind, taken in 1958.

CUMBERLAND NEWS,

SATURDAY, JAN. 25, 1947

An Old Local Industry

A good deal of research would no doubt be necessary to trace the oldest business in Carlisle, but the city is probably the only place in England, North of Staffordshire, where the old industry of manufacturing hand-made chains is still carried on. This, however, is a dying industry, as the hand-made chain has been almost entirely replaced by the electrically-welded product, although they are still made by Messrs Whitfield and Howe, Ltd., Lorne Street, for agricultural purposes, collieries and cranes. They also produce hames for horses, as well as clog irons. The firm was established as long ago as 1829, and when I was at their premises recently Mr J. Harrison explained that originally part of the work in Staffordshire was done by women, who took the iron from the works and made the links at home. The swivels were made later, and joined, by men. "But," said Mr Harrison, "women are now going in for 'softer' jobs. When the electrically-welded chain arrived about 20 years ago, it was produced so much cheaper that poorer wages resulted for the hand-workers, and that has had a lot to do with the industry's present position. Hand-made chains are infinitely stronger than the others, which are not made under the same even temperature throughout, and there are some chains with specially twisted links which it is impossible to make by electric welding."

Established by Joshua Whitfield in 1829 the firm was at first in Carlisle Square before moving to Mary Street. Joshua's son, John, submitted plans in September 1872 for a house and workshop on the newly laid out Lorne Street, to be known as Lorne Works, "for the purpose of manufacturing chains and caulkers". By 1895 it was William Whitfield & Sons and in 1899 the partnership was formed of Whitfield & Howe, Howe having been a coach builder. The firm continued coach building on Lowther Street.

Mrs Hilda Brown, great-granddaughter of the founder reminisced in 1971: "when my grandfather died [in 1895] he left his son John [my father] at the age of 20 to carry on the business which he did for some years, eventually selling it to Joseph Fidler. After a few years in retirement he was invited back as works manager and director, but finally retired on the death of Mr Fidler. James Harrison carried on the business for a while until he was forced to retire through illness and the Lorne Street works finally closed down". She went on to explain, "Hames, the steel casing round the collar used by dray horses, were also a profitable side of the business, but again, when the motor took the place of the horse, that side of the business declined. Caulkers, perhaps better knows as clog irons, were made to a special pattern for the district and were in demand until the war by makers of clogs". A change of use for Lorne Works was proposed in 1958 and the firm closed down soon after, the building being demolished for an extension to Pratchitts in the 1960s.

Top right: newspaper report on the firm.

Right: the view of the works from Randall Street in 1958.
Below: an 1880 advert for the original company.

xxx   ARTHUR'S DIRECTORY OF CARLISLE.

J. WHITFIELD & SON,
Chain, Hame, & Caulker Manufacturers,
Saddlers' and Cloggers' Ironmongery, &c.

Lorne Street, Denton Holme, CARLISLE.

SADDLE TREE PLATERS AND DEALERS IN SADDLE TREES.

TYER & CO

Left: a World War One group photograph of the Denton Holme workforce when 162 women and men were involved in war work.

Below: one of Tyer's patent locking points made by Tweedy's at Carlisle.

Bottom left: Tom Brown at his planing machine inside Tyer's works.

Bottom right: the works shown on the 1900 OS map.

Scotsman, Joseph Tweedy of J Tweedy & Co Engineers, Carlisle, patented a locking frame for railway signals in 1873. With increased workload new manufacturing premises on Garfield Street was given planning permission in 1875. The firm was taken over by Tyer & Co of London in 1898 and all production came to Carlisle. Robert Wilkinson Tweedy was managing director at Carlisle and with Mr Tyer's death in 1912 he became chairman. Tweedy lived at Wetheral and Norfolk Road moving to London four years before his death in 1916.

Signalling equipment from Carlisle went all over the world. The company continued at Denton Holme until 1927 and manufacturing was transferred to Keay's at Darlaston, Tyer & Co continuing into the 1950s. The Garfield Street site was used in later years for the storage of vehicles for the County Garage and more recently the development of Lewis Court named after a former MP for Carlisle.

Ashley Kendall, two images

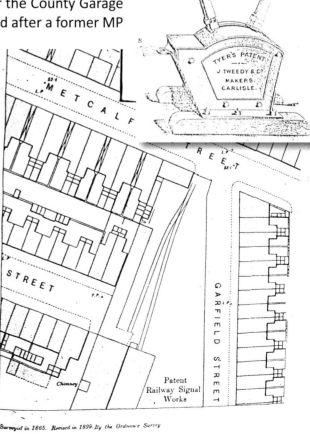

Carlisle Library, two images

ARCHITECTURE

Denis Perriam, four images

Above: Sir Robert Lorimer's house '**Tuethor**' for the Morton family at the corner of Empire Road and St James Road of 1922. The name reflected the time spent in the house from Tuesday to Thursday.

Above: Peter Dixon & Sons built housing on this street in the 1840s and the firm having its origins at Warwick Bridge, where there was a church by Pugin, this may be the reason for the choice of name.

Architects designing buildings for Denton Holme included some from Bradford and York. Only one, Maurice C Williams, was resident on St James Road when his daughter was born in 1888.

To pass planning regulations architects and builders had to submit plans for each building they constructed from 1856 so, for most of Denton Holme, plans exist in the Archive Centre. Few buildings are listed and while 'Tuethur' is one of the better houses, Sir Robert Lorimer's other factory blocks at Denton Hill are very utilitarian.

Above: architects such as Daniel Birkett used decorative brickwork to embellish their designs as with this building on Norfolk Street.

Below: as this factory block was designed by Carlisle architect, Henry Higginson, when it was converted to flats it was given the name Higginson's Mill. Another block at Holme Head has been called Johnston's Mill, named after the designing architect JW Johnston.

Below: some ordinary terraced houses were embellished and these in Charlotte Street had carved heads as keystones.

Findlay Stirling

SCULPTORS

Above: Rogerson's yard on Blencowe Street with Murrell Hill House in the background.

Above: some of Rogerson's gravestones from a billhead of 1903.

The reason for so many sculptors having yards in Denton Holme was the close proximity of the cemetery.

One of the foremost sculptors in Denton Holme was Thomas Nelson the business passing to James Nelson. The successor to that firm was Joseph Rogerson in 1901 he having been the former manager. He took Murrell Hill Cottage and the works extended along Blencowe Street.

Also on that street was Johnstone Brothers, William and Matthew, who had a yard alongside the railway. The partnership was dissolved in 1907 and William continued the business until he retired in 1916 offering the entire stock for sale with the machinery for manufacture.

Kirkpatrick & Nixon were monumental masons on Denton Street in 1886 when the partnership was dissolved and James Kirkpatrick carried on alone.

DJ Hill had a monumental masons yard on Denton Street opposite Robert Ferguson School but the site was required for housing development in the 1920s.

Left: Johnstone's yard on Blencowe Street.

Above right: the pulpit supplied by Nelson for St James Church.

Right: advertising stone for DJ Hill.

LEMONADE

Ashley Kendall

Findlay Stirling

Above: the Crown Works as it is today.

Left: William Underwood holds the horse's reigns of the firm's cart outside of the Crown Works, while another William Underwood is the driver.

Carlisle-born William Underwood returned to the city in 1880 to establish the firm of Underwood's Mineral Water Co and in 1881 the business was in Trafalgar Street. The move to Junction Street came in 1888 with new buildings but William died on 1 May 1889 aged 54 and his wife Frances was left to manage the business. She planned and built the Crown Works on Junction Street in 1899. Responsibility passed to eldest son John Ewart Underwood but he died in 1914. David Underwood took on the management of this and his own business in Maryport.

On the death of Frances in 1919, aged 84, the firm was for sale but it was saved as a going concern by Thomas Underwood. When bankruptcy threatened in 1925, Sarah Elizabeth Underwood, wife of Thomas, took on the business and oversaw the transfer to Peter Street in the 1930s. At a later date the firm was taken over by St Michael's of Eastriggs.

There was competition AH Noble having aerated water works on East Dale Street these premises becoming Batey & Sons by 1940.

Denis Perriam

Above: Noble had come to Carlisle in 1924 and set up his lemonade business on East Dale Street in 1926. He was bankrupt in 1939 and bottles like this are rare.

Above: bottle label for a special drink to celebrate the 1902 Coronation.
Right: advert from the 1902-03 *Carlisle Directory*.

SETTLED
AT
LAST !

What shall we Drink ?
Whose shall we Drink ?

Has long been the Question.

But, after A FAIR TRIAL, extending over a period of 20 years, the Public have given A POPULAR VERDICT in favour of

UNDERWOOD'S
❋ FAMOUS BEVERAGES. ❋

Manufacturer of Mineral Waters in Corks, Syphons, Screws, Patents, &c.

STONE GINGER, HOP BITTERS, FRUIT WINES, LIME JUICE, PEPPERMINT & ORANGE BITTER CORDIALS.

Hotel Keepers, Shop Keepers, &c., Write for Samples.   It will pay you ! Private Parties, Balls, &c., Catered for.

Address:—F. UNDERWOOD,

CROWN WORKS, CARLISLE.

CO-OP DEPOT

Donald Scott who worked for the Co-op said, "Gathered around a splendid cobbled yard were all the shops and back-up service that oiled the cogs of the giant Co-op machine. Employees entered the yard through a giant gateway that adjoined a shop front displaying a variety of Co-op headstones. Inside were stables and a harness room for the Co-op milk horses, Rolls Royce hearses for Co-op funerals and a stone-mason's shop. There was also a warehouse, joiner's shop, garage, coal yard, wholesale butcher's shop and bakery."

Above: Carlisle South End Cooperative Society bought Denton Mill in 1885 and rebuilt it in 1886. They then moved their flour mill from Botchergate to the new building. The yard and low building on the left became the Co-op funeral department where monumental masons worked.

Above: nearby Denton Mill was Nelson's Marble Works which was for sale in 1902. The site was acquired by the South End Co-op as their coal depot, accessed from Junction Street. Coal deliveries were by a siding which came off the Canal Branch and had previously served the Marble Works. Here the street delivery horses and drivers are posed for a photograph about 1905.

Below: land fronting Junction Street was acquired by the Co-op and it was here in 1913 that a Hygienic Bakery was built using flour from the mill to supply the many branches of the South End Co-op in and around Carlisle. The building is seen here during demolition in 1982 and beyond it the shoemaking department was also coming down.

Below: the bakery was still in full production in the 1950s with delivery vans taking the products as far as Appleby.

JOINERS AND TIMBER MERCHANTS

Bill Boak, two images

Above: the timber yard photographed in 1913 occupied where the present Anderson building is today and was served by a siding from the Canal Branch.

Right: Thomas Anderson went into partnership with James Graham in 1870. When Graham moved to Newcastle in 1885 Thomas Anderson took over and with his two sons traded as Thomas Anderson & Sons..

Timber Tade Journal

Above: in the 1860s James Graham had a timber yard where Lime and Elm Streets were built, hence the reason for the names.

Above: interior of Anderson's workshop in 1913. Much of the timber was imported from New Brunswick, Norway, Sweden, Russia, Canada and Gulf of Mexico.

Isaac Armstrong had a timber yard on Denton Street moving there from Lowther Street in 1865.

Carlisle architect, CJ Ferguson, chose George Black & Son, of Lorne Street, to carry out the timberwork for the restoration of Bamburgh Castle from 1896-1900. For this work a large model of the castle was made and this is on exhibition at the Castle with a label stating "it was made by Andrew Smith in 1900 in a warehouse at Lime Street, Carlisle", he being one of Black's workmen. But it seems to be earlier as the model was exhibited at the Royal Academy in 1896. Black retired in 1913 and work by the firm can be found in many Cumbrian buildings.

A successor may have been JW Hetherington & Sons who extended through to Sheffield Street and a woodyard in Thomas Street which was destroyed by fire in 1945. Another joinery firm was that of Messrs Bolton on East Dale Street.

Patt Honeyman

Above: timber wagon in Charlotte Street possibly on its way to Andersons.

Above: today Simpsons trade from Blencowe Street as joiners and undertakers.

THOMPSON'S COAL DEPOT

Carlisle Library

Ashley Kendall

Above: Samuel Jackson Binning had come to Carlisle from Newcastle in 1854 and in 1861 took over the sole agency in the city of Messrs Thompson, having married Isabella Thompson. It was he who managed the coal depot until his death in 1894 when his son [above] William Binning took over. On his death in 1936 Foster Bros took over the business.

Above: Major Thomas Charles Thompson of Milton Hall acting for Naworth Collieries, purchased a site on the corner of Thomas Street and Denton Street in 1870. The part nearest the railway became a coal depot for the collieries and the rest was developed for housing and a shop in 1885.

On the death of Thomas in 1888, by then a Lieutenant Colonel, he left the depot to his son CL Thompson. This shows the shop built by Thompson on the corner site when Thomas Minns had it. Today it has been converted into a house.

NAWORTH, BLENKINSOPP AND FEATHERSTONE COLLIERIES

Denis Perriam

Lord Carlisle's Railways . Brian Webb

Above: part of the letterhead for a bill sent from the coal agent to a purchaser.

Left: a private-owner wagon of the type used to deliver coal from the collieries to Denton Holme. Maria Thompson had the colliery lease from 1851 until her death in 1891 and Thomas was one of her sons. Isabella was also her daughter.

Carlisle Library

John Huggon

Above: a mission hall outing in Blencowe Street in 1925. Open-topped charabancs were popular for summer trips at that time.

Above: a Pratchitt's mark 1 steam lorry named Emperor of 1905. This was painted a rich deep red with black rectangular panels outlined in white. These had a vertical boiler as did the mark 2 version produced in 1906.

Ashley Kendall

Above: Robinson's newly delivered Austin van in the 1950s.

DENTON GARAGE
THOMAS ST.,
CARLISLE

PHONE 1163 · Proprietor— J. ARMSTRONG

PRESSUR

MAIN AGENT *for* JOWETT

**Private Cars and Commercial Vehicles
Body Building and Coach Painting**

MECHANICAL
OVERHAULS

Castrol
LUBREQUIPMENT
SERVICE

PETROL,
OILS, ETC.

John Huggon
Carlisle Journal, 24 May 1935

Above: 1935 advert for the Denton Garage giving an interior view. There is still a Denton Garage on Thomas Street.

Dennis Irwin

Above: Denton Tyres occupied the same site on Sheffield Street for many years. Recently, although keeping the name, they were taken over by Protyre. Newer arrivals include Kwik Fit on Junction Street.

Sundour Shuttle, Dec 1953

Above: a Morton lorry decorated to take part in the 1953 Coronation procession through Carlisle.

KENTMERE LTD

Left: the Kentmere Cardboard Box factory was close to the Caldew at the end of Lime Street next to the railway. There was a serious fire and this was the rebuilt factory in 1987.

Below: The box factory viewed from the river.

Kentmere was set up as a business in 1906 by two Windermere chemists with the sole object of producing photographic paper. They chose a name for the company, based at Stavely, which would reflect their location. In World War One the company was told to close paper production and instead they produced jam, the large kettles used for emulsion preparation were adapted for bulk jam making, using damsons from the Kendal area.

This was successful and they continued production after the war had ended, one order was for 100,000 jars. Diversifying again the company decided to expand with a cardboard box factory at Carlisle.

While Kentmere left Carlisle they still produce photographic paper and remain fiercely independent.

Left: photographic paper produced at Stavely near Kendal is still a popular product.
Below: at Carlisle the firm specialised in making cardboard boxes having started at English Damside and moved around until settling at the Denton Holme site, this advert being from 1952.

Kentmere Papers

YIELD DISTINCTIVE AND PERMANENT RESULTS.

PACK IT IN A BOX

There is no doubt that the presentation of goods to the buyer packed in an attractive box does count enormously.

WE ARE MAKERS OF CARDBOARD BOXES FOR ALL PURPOSES

PLEASE ASK FOR SAMPLES AND PRICES

KENTMERE, LTD.

LIME STREET, DENTON HOLME,

Telephone 606 **CARLISLE**

POST OFFICE

.**Above**: the post office when it was on the corner of Denton Street and East Nelson Street with William Gray as sub-postmaster. The lamp and lack of tramway suggest a late 1890s date. As well as postmaster, William Gray had a photographic business in the same premises and it seems his photographs are in the windows.

Right: the Denton Street pillar box which appears to be in the same position where it was erected in the late 1870s - and a Denton Holme postmark.

Above: Robinson's on Denton Street when this was the post office.

Below: the 1982 sorting office on Junction Street.

A post office was opened in Denton Holme on 2 April 1878 and this moved from one location to another on Denton Street. The pillar box remained in a fixed position and was joined by others on the corner of St James Road, one on Dalston Road, Holme Head and Junction Street. Land was acquired in the late 1940s for a parcels sorting office on Junction Street and the site adjoining this was chosen for a new sorting office which opened in 1982. With reorganisation Denton Holme is now without a post office.

Below right: sorting the morning mail at Morton Sundour's office in 1954.

INDUSTRIAL ESTATES

Denis Perriam

Above: Smith & Co relocated to a newly built office and workshop on Junction Street seen here for the opening on 14 December 1946.

Below: While the company has ceased trading their sign, an electric motor, was retained as an historic feature, recently removed.

Findlay Stirling, two images

Post-war development saw the setting up of Industrial Estates and the first fledgling one was at Murrell Hill along Junction Street. The GPO built their first sorting office there and Smith's Electricals relocated in 1946.

More recently brown-field sites have been chosen for council-built units, particularly Denton Holme Trade Centre of 1983, which is on land which was formally the Denton Holme Goods yard and Bourne House on a site on Milbourne Street previously a builder's yard.

In April 1983 the *Courier/Gazette* reported on the launch of the industrial units stating, " the development will protect existing employment and also promote new job opportunities in the area by providing the right sort of accommodation for both established and newly created businesses alike".

Right: the industrial units entered from Chapel Place on Milbourne Street. This land had been earmarked for the Inner Ring Road but with the abandonment of that scheme these units were commenced in 1982.

PUBLIC HOUSES

Denis Perriam

Left: 110 Denton Street was the Denton Inn, a beer house in 1867, later belonging to Iredale's Brewery, having stables and byres at the rear.

Henry Loughran, the licensee, was trying to sell in 1880. Rejections came for a full licence in 1885 and 1901.

There were various licensees before it came under Central Control ownership on 29 August 1916. Closure came on 17 October 1927 being converted into two shops.

Because of the late development of Denton Holme in the second-half of the 19th century there were few public houses allowed, the licensing authority by then having stricter control of drinking habits. There were complaints about the lack of such establishments but it made no difference to the sparse number.

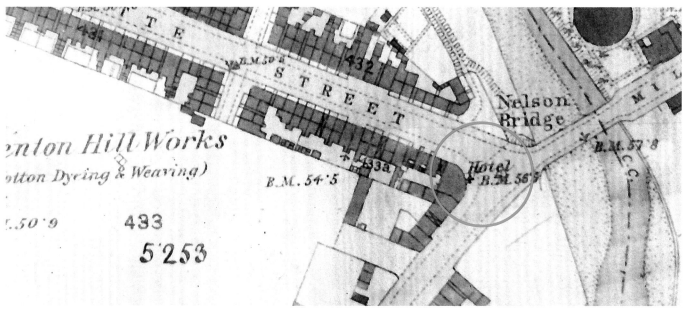

Above: the 1865 OS map shows the original site of the Nelson Bridge Hotel.

Right: as the building shown above was to come down to make way for the Viaduct the Nelson Bridge Hotel moved across the road to a former grocer's shop at the junction of Denton Crescent and Elm Street in 1875. This property had been compulsorily purchased by the railway and was sold by them to the Central Control Board in 1916. It remained open as the Nelson Bridge Inn until March 1971.

Carlisle Library, two images.

Left: there were three pubs on Milbourne Street and from the deeds the Milbourne Arms Hotel was first in 1852, John Norman the licensee advertising pigeon shooting that year. When offered for sale in January 1879 there was a rear quoiting ground.

Purchased by the Central Control Board on 17 August 1916 this became a 'Special Food Tavern' with off-sales. With the CDSMS sale on 22 May 1973 this became the property of Greenalls.

Floods in 2005 and 2015 damaged the interior but with refurbishment it reopened.

Right: the Spinners Arms on Milbourne Street took its name from the nearby Dixon's factory. It seems to have been an inn from the outset an inquest being held there in March 1858. This pub belonged to the Meadow Brewery and was let to various tenants until closure under the Central Control Board after purchase in 1916 from the Maryport Brewery.

Left: when offered for sale in September 1875 it was stated that the Wool Pack Inn had recently been granted a spirit licence. Under State Control this continued as a pub despite being opposite the Milbourne Arms. In the State sale in 1972 it was bought privately but by 1973 it was owned by Jennings Brewery.

They extended the pub in 1987. In 1997 it was re-named Biddy Mulligans and there was another name change in 2003 as The Knight Inn before eventual closure in 2008.

PRINCE OF WALES

Above: various tokens exist for the Prince of Wales Hotel and these may have applied to the bowling green or given as rewards for the return of crates and bottles. This one from the 1880s.

Left: the pub in 1902 before the brickwork was rendered. All that remains today are the railings.

Below: glass whisky flask for off-sales impressed with the pub name, dating from the 1890s.

Below right: fighting the fire on Christmas Eve 2008.

What had been built as terrace housing on the corner of Denton Street and Northumberland Street, at some time after 1853, was converted to a public house, named on the 1865 OS map as the *Prince of Wales*. Attached to this was a later bowling green, a match being advertised there on 1 April 1870. The pub was compulsorily purchased from the Carlisle New Brewery Co on 24 June 1916 by the Central Control Board.

Various modernisations were carried out under State ownership to make the building more uniform; the first in 1921 and the last in 1965. As part of the CDSMS sell-off on 8 May 1973 the pub became the property of John Smith & Co.

A decision was taken to close in 2004 and the derelict building was demolished after a fire with the option of building flats. As yet no further development has taken place.

CINEMA

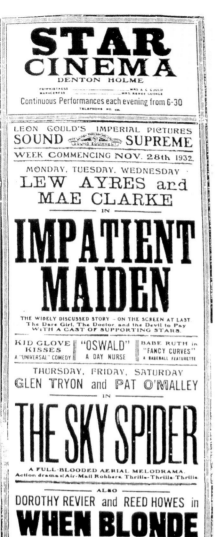

Above: Leon Gould, real name Charles Barrett Gould, had come to Carlisle from Chester-le-Street in 1911 to lease the Stanley Hall Picture House on Botchergate.

The Star Picture House [and Billiard hall] was built on part of the *Prince of Wales* bowling green, a restricted site between housing on Morley Street and Denton Street.

An application for a Cinematograph Act licence was made to the Watch Committee on 26 January 1912 by owner John Ferguson. After an inspection of the premises a licence was granted on 1 February 1912 to run to the end of that year and it opened the next day. Silent films were shown accompanied by a single pianist. One commentator stated, "this attracted factory workers and shop girls who didn't have to dress up to attend such places".

The first manager, Alf Norton, left in July and after closing for a fortnight for redecoration the picture house reopened on 26 July with Leon Gould in charge. As well as hiring in films Gould commissioned them - one being *Works & Workers of Denton Holme*.

Gould was able to purchase the property in 1922 and at his death in 1927 his wife, Annie, continued with assistance from daughter Renee and later her husband, Bertram George.

Sound was introduced in 1932 and the Star was leased to Graves Cinemas Ltd in 1933, the name changing to the Rex in 1938.

With increasing television viewing in Carlisle many cinemas closed and the Rex followed converting to Bingo on Boxing Day 1961 under the management of Bert George.

Right: *Carlisle Journal* 26 January 1962 headline.

Left: 1932 poster for the cinema featuring talkies.

Left: the entrance in the early 1920s when seats for adults were 2d, 3d and 6d; children were 2d and 3d.

Right: the basic interior of the viewing area at the same period.

INGLEWOOD

Archive Centre, Carlisle.

Left: Inglewood photographed for a sale catalogue in 1905.

Below: Thomas Williamson and wife Clara pose outside the front door with sons, Tom [left] and Joseph. Daughter Annie in the doorway has her children Arthur and Clara who died young.

Below left: Herbert Ramsden being congratulated by the Mayor and Mayoress having reached 100, watched by his sister Agnes Lowther who was 102. Both were residents of Inglewood Home when this was taken in 1984.

When a fire caused £1,000 of damage at Port Road Tannery in 1885, it was explained that Thomas Williamson "had entered the premises five years ago as a tenant of Mrs Mark of Causeway Head, Silloth, in succession to Mr Tinniswood". It was also stated in the *Carlisle Journal* that "Mr Williamson lives nearby". However he moved soon after to The Hollies on Norfolk Road. It was there in August 1892 that Annie Williamson went upstairs singing and in a dizzy fit fell down the stairs and was killed aged only 35.

Thomas remarried and having rebuilt the tannery he had Inglewood built with his initials on it and the date 1897. Tragically he also died there in 1904 aged 50 leaving his sons to carry on the business.

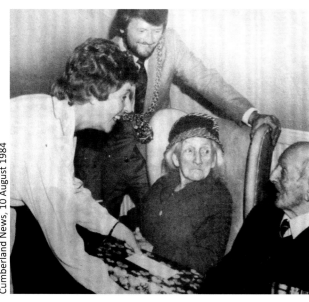

Cumberland News, 10 August 1984

Carlisle Library

GREYSTEAD

Above: Greystead viewed from Dalston Road in 2002. The gate and rails at the left are for the private Norfolk Road from which the house is accessed.

Above: sale notice for the house in 1926, Carr having moved to Dalston. It was bought by Ellwood Scott who was managing director of Scotts Leather works on Rome Street. When Scott died the house was again for sale.

Greystead was designed by William Johnstone in an Arts & Crafts style for the grandson of the founder of Carr's biscuits, William Theodore Carr, in 1911. The land had been purchased from the Ecclesiastical Commissioners on the understanding that the remaining fields between here and the Cemetery would not be built on. With his passion for cars and an engineering mind, Theodore had a garage built alongside in 1912 which had a turntable.

When the Longsowerby estate was to be built in 1919 Theodore was the only objector and while he withdrew this he was never very happy with his new neighbours.

Above: Theodore Carr in the car he designed as a three-wheeler and rebuilt in 1897. This was a steam vehicle which ran on petroleum.

Left: the author and his father George Perriam in the garden of Greysteads. This was on the occasion of the marriage in 1967 of Jean Perriam, daughter of George, and Frank Eastwood.

Right: on 15 September 1964 permission was granted to Mr & Mrs Desmond Potts for conversion from a house to a private hotel and it remains in that use today retaining the original house name with an added 's'.

WORLD WAR ONE

Ashley Kendall, two images

Denis Perri8am

Above: there were various 'hospital days' where flags were sold to raise money for war hospitals. This one shows the usual uniform for wounded soldiers - a blue jacket with white shirt and red tie.

Above: Murrell Hill House became a Red Cross auxiliary military hospital on 25 March 1915. This group photograph was taken in the grounds on 16 July 1916. The hospital had 28 beds increased to 40 by the time of closure on 27 March 1919. A total of 504 soldiers were treated with only one death.

Right: this group of VAD volunteers has been photographed at Teasdale's factory, the managing director being Edward Wheatly Pigg who sits in the car. These men would meet trains carrying the wounded and transport them to various military hospitals around the city.

Left: workers in Pratchitt's works switched production to making, amongst other items, shell cases seen in the foreground.

Below left: Tyer's also switched production to munitions work and here are a group of mostly women in 1917 involved in this work, each displaying their triangular 'On War Service' badges.

Below: each street, or group of streets, held peace celebrations in 1919, these being residents commemorating the event with a street party in Milbourne Crescent.

Archive Centre, Carlisle.

Bill Boak

ALLOTMENTS

Denis Perriam

Above: the Richardson Street allotments which thrive today.

The *Carlisle Journal* 15 December 1893 reported on a meeting of the proposed Denton Holme Allotments at Blencowe Street Mission Hall "with a view to ascertaining the nature of the demand for garden allotments under the Act of 1887". Available was a five and a half acre corporation owned field on Dalston Road but 20 or 40 persons would have to apply before this could be used.

The scheme was abandoned in favour of one and a half acres on the Holme Head road which the newspaper stated in March 1896, "Mr Constable, acting on behalf of Messrs Ferguson Bros, has had laid out and well fenced". These were described as the Denton Holme Allotments and 35 plots were available. By July there were 54 members and there was great competition between them. Chicken runs were also provided for workmen at the factory.

In celebrating the 12th AGM the *Carlisle Journal* stated that Fergusons had given more land and there were 109 plots with 123 members and 14 waiting for plots. By 1913 there was also a garden pavilion.

Other allotments followed as a result of war and in December 1916 the newspaper reported on the Murrell Hill ones laid out on railway land. In 1919 there was an evening tea and dance organised by the Junction Street Allotment Society.

With the construction of the Longsowerby estate more land was used by Fergusons in 1922 for allotments, they leasing this from the corporation. On 14 July 1922 minutes reported the widening of Cemetery Lane with allotments on either side of it. In 1929 this was referred to as an acre on Diggle Road to Cemetery Road.

Other allotments are behind Richardson Street relocated to part of the former football pitch as the site near Ferguson Bros was subject to industrial development.

Carlisle Library

Above: the Home Food Culture movement saw more land being used as allotments during World War One

Right: Joseph Cartwright, a worker at Ferguson Bros, had a pigeon loft on Junction Street allotments and was a keen member of the Eden Vale Homing Society, Eden Vale being the name given to the printing department at Ferguson Bros.

Holme Headings, September 1950.

LONGSOWERBY

Archive Centre, Carlisle

FRONT ELEVATION

Left: the design by City Surveyor, Henry Marks, in December 1919 for the proposed Longsowerby houses.

The plan was approved with a note to say the timber cladding was cancelled but it was allowed on other houses in the scheme.

Previously in 1895 the land was used as a 9 - hole golf course known as St James Golf Club.

The 1919 Housing Act was intended to provide good quality working-class housing and Carlisle took this very seriously, Jean Turnbull stating, "it was one of the first local authorities to prepare a detailed housing plan in 1919". As well as council houses at Bousteads Grassing, Denton Street and Stanwix a new estate was planned at Longsowerby.

This was a field forming part of Newlaithes Grange belonging to the Priory of St Mary which passed to the Dean & Chapter and then the Ecclesiastical Commissioners. Because the land was sold to the corporation by the church the streets reflected the former ownership.

John Hugeon

Above: no provision had been made in the estate for shops and this Coop store was opened as an afterthought in 1929 on Waldegrave Road.

Above: because of the former ownership of Longsowerby some of the streets were named after recent and past Bishops of Carlisle.

Right: looking into the estate from Dalston Road.

Denis Perriam

SPECIAL OCCASIONS

Ashley Kendall

Above: hundreds of poor children queue at the Congregational Church to receive Christmas presents on 23 December 1911. Each eligible child was given a ticket and Thomas Bulman has redeemed his for a sword as he crosses the road.

Above: the same day at the head of the queue where helpers regulate the flow into the church hall. These photographs were taken by R Black & Son.

Carlisle Library, two images.

John Huggon

Above: the annual St James Church procession passes Denton Hill Works on Lorne Crescent in 1925.

Above: children with their Silver Jubilee tins on Norfolk Street, opposite Carricks, in 1935. Celebrations were held to mark 25 years of George V's reign.

John Zeller

Left: Empire Day 1939 at Robert Ferguson School. Margaret Underwood leads with Jean Haughan carrying the Union Jack and behind her John Zeller.

James Hope wrote to the council on 14 May 1907 to say he was "strongly opposed to the ... Education Committee to spend £90 on the purchase of flags for the celebration of Empire Day in schools in the city". This he thought a "sheer waste of money ... to inoculate into the minds of the children a spurious form of Patriotism - Jingoism and militarism which is an obstacle to the progress of the world".

FIRE-FIGHTING

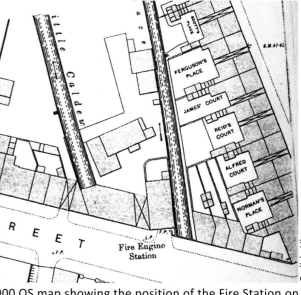

Above: The 1900 OS map showing the position of the Fire Station on Junction Street..

Above left: the 1973 fire at Teasdale's sweet factory.

Left: the larger mills had their own fire-fighting teams with regular competitive exercises. A Ferguson team were in a contest at Darlington in 1882. The team are seen here with a new trailer pump.

Above: men from the Auxiliary Fire Service outside the Junction Street station which was brought back into use during the war. The man in the boiler suit was John Hetherington who lived above the station.

Below: the 1884 foundation stone at Junction Street showing this was intended for the Carlisle Volunteer Fire Brigade.

Left: the Junction Street Fire Station cost £517 and opened on 23 January 1885. A manual fire engine, fire escape the other apparatus was kept there, the ground floor also having a reading and committee room. Above was the caretaker's accommodation. In later years it was put to other uses.

LAW AND ORDER

Trevor Grahamslaw

Denis Perriam, two images

Above: PC 53 in the 1870s, a photograph taken by Hesket Andrews in his Sheffield Street studio.

Top left: Parliamentary elections for St Cuthbert's Ward held at Charlotte Street church on 14 July 1905. Carlisle City Police are on duty to ensure all went well on the day including an older PC 53.

A CAUTION.

TO THE EDITOR OF THE CARLISLE JOURNAL.

Sir,— Will you allow me, through the medium of your valuable paper, to call the attention of the public and police to the following disgraceful circumstance?

On Tuesday, the 27th inst., a little girl about eight years of age, whose parents reside in Denton Holme, was returning from Milbourne Street by the Frigate Lonning. When near to Nelson's Cottage she was accosted by a man who promised her a penny if she would go a walking with him past the new church (St. James's). Fortunately, another man came up at the time, who apparently knew the other one, as he stopped and spoke to him a short time, which enabled the child to get away. She ran home and told her mother, who immediately went to look after the man. When near to the same place she saw the miscreant taking off another child no bigger than her own.

Upon seeing the woman approaching he ran away, and getting on the railway was soon lost to sight, but not before the woman was near enough to identify him if she should meet him again.

What makes the matter more serious the same man is known to have made two other attempts upon children in our neighbourhood. He is a respectably dressed man, rather tall, slender, and deeply pitted with small pox.

I trust that by your insertion of this it may cause a look-out to be kept, and that the unmanly brute may soon meet the reward his base conduct entitles him to.

COMMUNE BONUM.

Denton Holme, March 30th.

Right: A policeman ponders evidence in Norfolk Terrace in the 1960's.

Carlisle Library

Left: the *Carlisle Journal* 1 April 1870 contained a letter of warning showing that sexual crimes were prevalent in the Victorian period.

SMASHING—WE'VE GOT A REAL POLICE BOX TO PLAY WITH!

Carlisle Journal, 8 February 1963.

Left: policing in 2018: a police van in Milbourne Street.

Right: police on the beat would regularly report in from police boxes at strategic points - this one (which had been knocked over) was on the corner opposite the Congregational Church.

ARTISTS

Sundour Shuttle December 1938

Above: Alastair Morton at work

Above: William Edward Tyler by Paul Greville Hudson in 1908 when he was living on Nelson Street and then Dalston Road.

William Edward Tyler was born at Bridgnorth in 1871 and came to Carlisle as a carpet designer for Morton Sundour in 1900. As an artist he exhibited atmospheric landscape views at the Royal Society of British Artists and the Royal Institute of Oil Painters. Returning to his native county by 1920 he continued as a designer and died at Bridgnorth in 1930.

Glasgow Museum

Above: interior view of 12 Norfolk Road by Bratby painted for the Seasons Exhibition at the Tate.

Alastair Morton was the Joint Managing Director of Morton Sundour and was a talented designer many of his works being in the Victoria and Albert Museum.

In the painting on the left by John Randall Bratby the figure on the right is councillor TL Macdonald and the woman is Bratby's wife Jean, holding in her arms their son David.

The artist stated that the councillor "is representative of the autumn of life, Jean is representative of the summer and David is representative of the spring, winter is represented by the oil stove".

In the background, Bratby wrote, was his studio, "an old Fire Service Control Room with a concrete roof and brick walls". This was painted in the winter of 1956.

He was born at Wimbledon studying at Kingston School of Art and the Royal College of Art 1951-54. In his DNB entry Andrew Lambirth said of Bratby, "he depicted the seedier aspects of his surroundings and would be found... painting a dustbin or setting up his easel in a lavatory". He began exhibiting at the Royal Academy in 1954 being elected a member in 1971.

On 1 September Bratby was appointed a tutor at Carlisle College of Art. He lived with his wife in a council owned flat at 12 Norfolk Road.

Also living on Norfolk Road was AG Tennant Moon a fellow pupil at the RCA before becoming principal of the College of Art.

Tullie House Museum and Art Gallery Trust two images

John Randall Bratby 1928-1992 self portrait 1954.

JOSEPH SIMPSON

Carlisle Library, two images

Denis Perriam

Left: a self-portrait etching in later life. In the 1930s Robert Forrester described him: tall, well-built... bald head and fresh complexion" with a friendly manner.

Top right: the artist's birthplace on St James Road, Poplar Villas.

Right: a posthumous exhibition was held at Tullie House in 1939 where 168 works were on show.

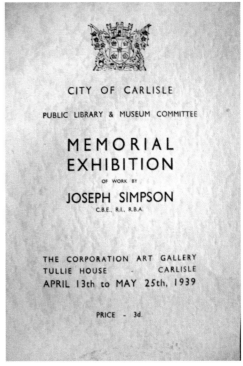

CITY OF CARLISLE

PUBLIC LIBRARY & MUSEUM COMMITTEE

MEMORIAL
EXHIBITION
OF WORK BY
JOSEPH SIMPSON
C.B.E., R.I., R.B.A.

THE CORPORATION ART GALLERY
TULLIE HOUSE - CARLISLE
APRIL 13th to MAY 25th, 1939

PRICE - 3d.

Joseph William Simpson, born 17 July 1878, was the son of Joseph who was a corn merchant, and a talented watercolour painter. His birthplace was opposite St James Church where he was baptised on 22 September 1878. With his father bankrupt in 1887 the family had to move to Myddleton Street but this did not prevent Joseph receiving a private education. At 15 he went to work in the Ordnance Survey office in Portland Square. In his spare time he attended classes at the School of Art under Herbert Lees, where he became a pupil teacher.

In December 1898 he was stated to have "recently left this city to study in Edinburgh" and in 1899 he exhibited at the RSA. Soon after 1901 he left for London where he married in 1905 his profession given as an artist. As a professional he painted many famous people but preferred the medium of etching being sought after as an illustrator. After a period in the trenches in 1918 he was made Official War Artist attached to the RAF and many of his aircraft studies are in the Imperial War Museum. He spent the rest of his life in London where he died on 30 January 1939.

Stephen White

ORIGINAL WATER-COLOUR
BY JOSEPH SIMPSON, C.B.E., R.B.A.
PRESENTED BY LADY CHANCE. 1930.

Left: Simpson's design for Thurnam's 1929 calendar. The subject, Sir Wilfred Lawson, was one of the two MPs for Carlisle with Robert Ferguson and hence the link with Lady Chance.

Right: portrait by Simpson of Sir Frederic Chance who was chairman and managing director of Ferguson Bros at Holme Head.

Fereguson Centenary Book

PHOTOGRAPHERS

Denis Perriam, three images.

Above and centre: Heskett Andrews may have at one point shared his studio with his son-in-law, John Warwick, until Andrews moved into the city centre and Warwick remained.

Far right: Horace William Smith, born in Scotland in 1861, was a photographer living at 42 Cumberland Street by 1883. He was a photographer working on his own account in 1911.

The earliest Denton Holme photographer was James Mundell 1814-1880 who was born in Kirkudbright and after being a schoolmaster in the Cockermouth area was a grocer at Thursby in 1861. By 1866 he was manager of the Caledonian Photographic Co, Denton Street having previously worked for the photographer Matthew Fisher in the city centre. Mundell lived on Charlotte Street and was still living in Carlisle in 1871, but was a photographer in Silloth by 1875. When he died he was living on Myddleton Street.

Hesket Andrews 1838-1894 was born in Wigton and in 1871 was at Denton Hill as a factory warehouseman. By 1874 he was at 46 Sheffield Street and a photographer. In 1879 he build a new studio on Devonshire Street. Later he lived at Maryport and died at Wigton.

Below right: a photograph taken for William Gray of Denton Street.
Below: one of the Denton Holme photographs taken by Joseph Monk showing the Coop Coal Depot on Junction Street.

Ashley Kendall

Ian Moonie

Ashley Kendall

Above: Edward Steele worked at Ferguson Bros but was also an amateur photographer. This is a birthday party inside his house on Freer Street in the 1920s. He was one of the first to make large format colour transparencies in Carlisle in the 1930s.

Above left: Thomas J Haughan was born at Carlisle in 1867 and was living on Charlotte Street in 1871, his father being a miller at Denton Mill. By 1891 he was at Silloth and must have been at the Viaduct Studio before Joseph Monk

Left: Reigate born Joseph Monk 1852-1932 was at 19 Cumberland Street in 1884. By 1893 he had the Viaduct Studio and was there until 1924.

Denis Perriam

John Warwick 1855-1926 was born in Carlisle and by 1881 was a printer's compositor. In that year he married Elizabeth the daughter of Heskett Andrews and was a photographer at 46 Sheffield Street by 1884 so used his father-in-law's former studio. While he was still in business there in 1893 he was living at Wetheral. He moved his studio to Lowther Street in 1895 and then Warwick Road before retiring to Silloth by 1911.

A patent for a camera slide with hinged shutter was awarded to JA Halhead of Denton Street in 1888. Thomas Hodgson 1860-1937 from Huddersfield was described as a photographer when living with his parents at 31 Sheffield Street in 1881.

John Banks, aged 60, a photographer of Caldew Street was rescued from drowning in the Caldew in June 1930. The son of James Kirkpatrick, monumental mason, was Thomas living with his parents in 1891 at 8 Trafalgar Street, his occupation given as photographer, one of his photographs has a Denton Street address.

Clifford Vero had been a photographer in the city centre before World War One.
Later he was manager of his father-in-law's drapery business (Tom Dobson) in Denton Street. The Denton Studios at 55 & 57 Denton Street were being advertised in 1967.

Special thanks to Ian Moonie in the production of these two pages.

Right: Thomas Story born in 1858 was an assistant to the photographer, Benjamin Scott, when he took this photo from the top of Dixon's Chimney in 1887. By 1903 Story was the professional operator for William Gray on Denton Street.

Mary Burgess Collection

THE CULLENS

Babs Cullen

Left: Babs Cullen as a youngster in Denton Holme clutching her favourite toy.

Right: the 1994 book which Babs wrote about Denton Holme. On the cover Babs Cullen stands between her father and Willie Kendal at the butchers shop at the corner of Norfolk Street and Denton Street. The Ca*rlisle Journal* 22 January 1926 shows this property sold to GW Cullen shortly before this photograph was taken.

A Denton Holme Childhood

Babs Cullen

Christened Edith Bell Cullen, Babs, as she preferred to be called, was born at Harker but at an early age came to live in Denton Holme. In the book on her childhood she wrote…. "immediately after being demobbed from the army, my dad, George and his brother Dick joined their father, George Cullen senior, in the family butcher business in Carlisle's Covered Market".

George William Cullen married Edith May Hodgson on 10 August 1920 at St Michael's Stanwix. They settled in a pretty little cottage at Harker.

Babs wrote, "An opportunity eventually arose for dad to acquire his uncle Joe's butcher shop at the corner of Denton Street and Norfolk Street… the old chap decided that the time had come to call it a day. Included in the purchase were two houses, one of them being partly over the shop, while the other was immediately in Norfolk Street…. so we left Harker and moved to Denton Holme".

Cumberland News, Friday 11 November 1994.

● **IN PRINT:** Babs Cullen shows off her book

Babs' book takes trip down memory lane

CHILDHOOD memories of life in Carlisle's Denton Holme form the basis of a new book out this week.

Written by Babs Cullen, the book takes a trip down memory lane to Denton Holme between 1920 and 1940.

Babs appealed through The Cumberland News for old photographs. The book includes pictures of shops long gone from

By Sue Crawford

the once bustling area, the slaughterhouse in Devonshire Walk, Holme Head bay and the textile works and old faces from the past.

Babs, who now lives near Kirkby Stephen, wrote the book under her maiden name. Her married name is Gubbins.

Her father George Cullen

opened a butcher's shop in 1938. He later opened a second shop in the market.

"I've wanted to do this book for a long time. It's been an interesting experience," she said.

● The book is available in Carlisle through W H Smith Woods Booksellers, John Watts coffee shop and the Lanes library.

ICE-CREAM, FISH & CHIPS

Babs Cullen

John Huggon, two images

Above: Pieri's shop on Denton Street before World War Two. The ice cream sold here was made in a small factory off Junction Street seen in the photograph below right.

Above: the interior of Pieri's fish and chip shop on Northumberland Street with the elaborate tiled ranges. Left to right are seen Tom Underwood, Alfredo Pieri and Rosie who was Alfredo's sister. Alfredo was unlucky being interned in World War Two as an Italian national and drowned when internees were to be transported to Canada. The ship was attacked and sunk by a German U-boat in the Atlantic on 2 July 1940.

Winnie Pieri (daughter in law) to Alfredo tells a story - At the age of 19 in 1941 she re-opened the closed fish and chip shop, employing two people to run it. She recalls that when the Rex cinema show finished each night they would make up 30 or 40 threepenny bags of chips for the rush of cinemagoers. One night only six weeks after opening she was at the cinema and left early to get back to the shop before the rush only to find there had been a fat fire and the range was ruined.

Above: ice cream cart decorated for a special occasion. This is outside the building which is now the office for Mountelm on Junction Street. Holding the reigns is Alfredo Pieri in this 1930s photograph with Joseph Pieri in the overall on the right. Originally this was a hand cart but was modified to be pulled by a pony.

Today the only Pieri shop to remain is on Northumberland Street but there are other fast food outlets offering fish & chips.

Barry Beckett

Above: an unknown helper [left], owner John Beckett, his wife Ethel and daughter Joyce stand outside their fish & chip shop on Denton Street. The decorations are for the Jubilee of 1935. Mr Becket had bought the shop from the Renucci family.

Right: Children pose outside Luigi Corrieri's fish and chip shop on Milbourne Crescent there until it's 1970s demolition.

Ashley Kendall

SHOPS

Above: Mrs Coulthard at the shop doorway of her newsagents on Nelson Street in 1904. Customers might have been enticed inside by the postcards in the window.

Above: Cogan's in Viaduct Buildings on Randall Street making full use of the outside of the shop to advertise the newspapers they sold. Tobacco products are seen in the window and the pole and sign shows they were also hairdressers.

Right: with little external advertising Johnstons on the corner of Cumberland Street relied on the shop window display.

Right: Reays newsagents on Denton Street made sure that the tobacco products they sold were well displayed inside. Ada Reay stands behind the counter. This was the last newsagent on Denton Street closing in 2014 to be replaced by a Turkish barber. This only leaves McCrea on Norfolk Street.

SHOPS

Ashley Kendall, two images.

Above: seeing what was for sale was all important to Annie Bowes with her fruit shop on Denton Street.

Stephen Dickinson

Left: signs helped to advertise what was sold inside like this pestle and mortar outside Bowmans Chemist on Denton Street.

Right: putting your name on bottles ensured they were returned and advertised the business.

Carlisle Library

Above: loyalty rewards were in use at the Coop and in the Red Stamp Store on the corner of Thomas Street. Joyce Lawson and John Smith are ready to serve customers and give out stamps.

GENTS·PRICE·LIST.

HAIRCUTTING	1/-
BOYS do	10d
SHAVING	6d
SHAMPOOING	1/-
SINGEING	10d
FACE MASSAGE	2/6
RAZOR SET	1/6
NECK SHAVING	3d

Above: The 1930s pricelist set in an Art Deco stained-glass frame for Lewthwaites.
Right: Lewthwaite used the traditional sign of blood and bandages to show that his shop was a barber.

Denis Perriam

SHOPS

Ashley Kendall

Left: Armstrong had a fish mongers shop on Denton Street and in 1951 Tom Armstrong sharpens his knife ready to fillet fish. At the time of this photo Tom was 64 but he kept on working long after retirement. He died in 1967 aged 80.

Below: Henry Edmondson was a boot maker at 25 Northumberland Street in 1905 and this was taken not long after that.

Babs Cullen

Below: the Wheeler grocery shop at the corner of North Street and Denton Street, Holme Head. There were a number of such corner shops in Denton Holme.

Below: William Morrow's butchers on Denton Street which was empty for many years before being converted into a house. This was just one of many butchers in Denton Street over the years.

David Young

Jeanne Perriam

CLUBS, SOCIETIES & ASSOCIATIONS

Above: the Denton Holme Children's Band, who were filmed by Paramount in October 1933 on parade at the Castle before they went to London to play in front of Queen Mary on 10 November. A crowd of 15,000 waited in Court Square to see their return. Here they are posed at Morley Street School with their bandmaster Mr DeColt.

Above: a Conservative Working Men's Recreational club was set up in 1878 at first in St James School before moving to premises on Nelson Street, seen here. A rival Denton Holme Labour Club closed in 1929.

There were many different organisations which flourished in Denton Holme. As well as recreational clubs there were a number of bands one being the Caldew Vale Silver Band, another being the Denton Hill Band at Morton Sundour. The South Vale Hornets had their own 'Art Union' when prizes were drawn in 1894. A South Vale Reading Room existed in 1869. There was also a Denton Holme District Nursing Association employing a nurse and a list of rules was published in 1892. Church organisations included the Boys Brigade and a Young People's Fellowship. The Magnet Cocoa Room was set up on Nelson Street in 1879 along with the 'British Workmen' principle as an alternative to the pub. The *Carlisle Journal* reported on 14 February 1879, "a commodious house which recently opened as a grocers is now being fitted up by a number of gentlemen in the Denton Holme district as a cocoa room". An ornamental lamp was erected over the door by the Ladies Committee of the Temperance Association. The Royal Observer Corps used a house on Norfolk Road as their HQ which had been commandeered in World War Two, but with a move to a new site in 1963 this was surplus to the Air Ministry requirements and is now 'The Laurels', a residential care home.

Above: the full company of the 4th Carlisle Boys Brigade, probably at Morton in the 1920s.

Above: led by a pipe band the Boys Brigade march past the church in parade.

HOLME HEAD RECREATION

FERGUSON · BROS: LTD
have laid out this land for
employees & public alike.
DUMPING RUBBISH & PLAYING
GAMES (FOOTBALL CRICKET &c) IS FORBIDDEN
Anyone causing damage will be
prosecuted.

Planning permission was given to Ferguson Brothers to lay out the Bridge Terrace bowling green in 1880, although it was thought to date from 1872. It was again re-laid and extended in 1893 with a reopening ceremony. There seems to have been more than bowling with mention of quoits in 1880.

Built at the same time was a Coffee Tavern and Reading Room opened in January 1882. The tavern was on the ground floor with the reading room above. There was a grocery shop adjoining and the grocer was also the custodian of the tavern. The tavern was replaced by a dining hall in 1912 but the reading room was still in use in 1949 and the building has been put to various uses since then. A planning application to convert this to a dwelling in July 1975 for Carrington Vyella was approved.

Denis Perriam, all images.

Above: the 1882 Coffee Tavern provided for Ferguson Bros workers built to the designs of George Dale Oliver.

Top right: a surviving sign for the recreational use of land alongside the river.

Right: winners of the Dalziel shield for bowling in 1904 posed at Holme Head green.

WEST END BOWLING CLUB

Above: an early enamelled club badge.

Left: a match in progress in the 1920s, Goschen Road behind.

Below: history of the club written in 1990

An official launch of the West End Club was held on 4 December 1889 in the schoolroom next to St James Church. Agreement had been reached with the Ecclesiastical Commissioners to lease a field next to Goschen Road for the green.

A NEW BOWLING GREEN FOR CARLISLE.

The West End Bowling Green, which has been recently constructed at Murrell Hill, in this city, was opened on Friday afternoon by the Mayor (Mr. R. Forster). The green is pleasantly situated between Goschen Road and Norfolk Road. It has been neatly enclosed, and a substantial pavilion has been erected on the east side. The turf was obtained from Maryport. There was a good gathering of members and friends, including Mr. Nathan Palmer (president of the Club), Mr. J. G. Forster (secretary), Mr. J. Hurst (treasurer), Mr. J. Hewitson Brown, Mr. Joseph Gibson, Mr. Rudd, Mr. Tweddle, Mr. L. Asquith, Mr. R. T. Hetherington, Mr. John Slack, Mr. W. Johnson, Mr. S. Ferguson, and others. The PRESIDENT, in calling upon the Mayor to open the green, said a provisional committee had been appointed at a meeting on the 6th October for the purpose of forming a bowling club for the West End. They succeeded in getting the present site from the Ecclesiastical Commissioners, but if their secretary had charged solicitors' fees for every letter he wrote on the subject they would have had an enormous bill to pay—(laughter)—and would not have been able, as they now were, to open the green free of debt. (Cheers.) The green had to be conducted entirely on teetotal principles; no intoxicants would be sold on the ground, and no member would be allowed to bring any, as they were all capable of spending a pleasant evening without stimulants. It was chiefly through the hard work of Mr. Hurst, their treasurer, that they had been able to pay every bill sent in without borrowing money from anyone. The place, with the pavilion, had cost £350, and the capital had been raised by £1 shares. Consequently most of the members were shareholders; and those who were not would regret it, as it was a safe investment at 5 per cent. The membership was limited to eighty, and there were now more than seventy members. The Club was non-political; and he was proud of the position he held as its president. The Committee had been fortunate in securing Joseph Rowell as greenkeeper, a man who understood and took a pride in his work.

With costs estimated at £350, shares to the value of £200 had already been sold and 60 people had indicated their willingness to become members.

The club flourishes today.

Centenary of West End Bowling Club 1890 - 1990

Carlisle Library

Above: the opening report in the *Carlisle Journal* 3 June 1890.

Denis Perriam, three images

Right: the green and pavilion with Goschen Road in the background in the late 1920s.

SPORT

Pratchitt's Centenary Book

Above: when the Denton Holme Cricket, Quoit & Football Club had their inaugural meeting in St James School room in April 1878 it was stated matches were held in the "field rented from Mr Birney which is at the side of the lane leading to the cemetery from Denton Holme".

This was later Richardson Street and from then on football was played there including Pratchitt's team in 1934.

Carlisle Library

Above: the Richardson Street field below St James Church was the venue for annual sports. This may have been the field that Fergusons rented to Mr Birney and had been in use for sports since 1878.

Holme Hesdings, September 1949.

Sundour Shuttle, December 1937.

Above: Morton Sundour set aside part of the gardens of Murrell Hill House as a recreation ground for workers in 1927. As well as a bowling green there were tennis courts. Here the bowling green is in use in 1937.

John Huggon

Above: sports day refreshments at Richardson Street in 1925.

Cumberland News

Above: the annual Holme Head Works sports is watched by a large crowd in 1935. In this race the jockeys were all ex-servicemen. Houses on Richardson Street can be seen on the left with Longsowerby council houses in the distance.

ST JAMES PARK

Denis Perriam

Above: the bowling green and bower at St James Park which has been in use since 1936.

Ashley Kendall

Above: the 1936 sunken garden behind the bower in an early colour photograph by Edward Steele incorporating the the architect's watercolour design.

A five acre site below St James Church between Colville Terrace and Norfolk Street, originally belonging to the Earl of Lonsdale, was acquired by Messrs Teasdale as their recreation ground for workers at the factory.

Dennis Irwin

Above: the children's play area in the park.

In 1934 they sold this to the city council for £2,000 inclusive of hard tennis courts and children's playground with swings and roundabout.

A wooden hut was replaced with a bower for a municipal bowling green which was laid out and opened by the Mayor on 30 April 1936. This was to be a recreation ground for the inhabitants of the Denton Holme and St Cuthbert's wards. The park included a sunken garden and a refurbished play area.

Later the tennis courts gave way to five-a-side football and next to this a BMX track. For some years there were annual fun days in the park

Above: one of the fun days in the park.

WORLD WAR 2

Mary Eite

Above: Denton Holme platoon of Dad's Army in a show of strength at their Morley Street School HQ. They manned a tank trap at the cemetery and another at Denton Holme in case the enemy used the river bank.

David Hay

Above: Robert Ferguson boys in their gas masks.

Below: volunteer fire fighters and drivers somewhere in Denton Holme, going to help in the Liverpool blitz.

Below: peace celebrations for VE Day in Colville Terrace, the tables and forms being borrowed from Teasdale's canteen.

Denis Perriam

Above: Auxiliary Fire service men with their fire engine fitted with restrictor and white edged mudguards. They are posed behind Morton's laboratory on Lorne Crescent.

In WW2 factories went into wartime production. Larger houses were taken into military service, Murrell Hill House being used by the Army and ATS. A school of wireless telegraphy was set up in the Congregational Church schoolroom, Dixon's chimney also acted as an aerial for signals.

The number of allotment plots increased in a 'Dig for Victory' campaign. Many residents joined the forces and one fatality was Sergeant

Barry Beckett

Pilot Hylton Cullen of Denton Street who died when his parachute failed to open. Ironically parachutes were being made at Morton's.

Right: with so much industry in Denton Holme there was a fear of enemy bombing. Even today the Emergency Water supply signs are still to be seen where firemen had access to fill their pumps.

Findlay Stirling

MARGOT WHITE

Above: Margaret Cairns White

Above: William Joyce in blackshirt uniform.

Born in Manchester on 14 July 1911, Margaret Cairns White came to Carlisle when her father got a job at Morton Sundour. In 1917 they were living on Nelson Street, so Margot, as she preferred, was brought up in Denton Holme and went to school in the city. Leaving school she got a job as a secretary at Sundours.

Interested in politics from an early age, at 22 she joined the Carlisle Branch of the British Union of Fascists in 1933. Attractive and vivacious, a good-time girl, outgoing and feminine she spent her time fleeing boredom. Margot attended a Fascist meeting at Dumfries on 7 February 1935 to see William Joyce speak and she joined him soon afterwards in Manchester. Joyce divorced his first wife in 1936 and asked Margot to

Above: the house at 63 Nelson Street where the White family lived.

marry him with a marriage on 13 February 1937. When Joyce founded the National Socialist League in 1937 Margot became assistant treasurer.

With war imminent the couple were advised to leave London and they were in Berlin when war was declared. They offered their services to the Nazi regime Joyce becoming a radio propagandist, nicknamed 'Lord Haw Haw', on 18 September 1939 with call sign 'Germany Calling, Germany Calling'. On 3 October Margot made her first broadcast being dubbed 'Lady Haw Haw'. Both became German subjects on 26 September 1940. After an affair and living separately the Joyces divorced on 12 August 1941 only to remarry on 11 February 1942. When captured at Flensburg on 28 May 1945 Joyce was charged with treason and was hanged in 1946. Margot was treated leniently and was released spending her last days in London where she died in 1972 having regained British citizenship.

Right: meeting of the Carlisle Blackshirts in 1935 with Margot on the front row third from right.

Left: the British public never saw Joyce during his propaganda broadcasts and this is a contemporary representation of him.

INNER RING ROAD

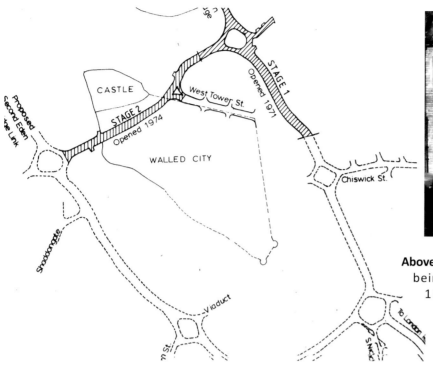

Above: Jim Barnes of the Carlisle Preservation Society being interviewed by Border Television in 1974 opposite Charlotte Street church. The society campaigned successfully to scrap the Ring Road scheme but could not save Charlotte Street.

Above: the Inner Ring Road as planned, the shaded area being that carried out and the dotted line the part proposed but later abandoned.

Denis Perriam, all images.

A plan for a Carlisle Inner Ring Road was drawn up in 1967. This was to be completed in a number of stages to minimise traffic disruption and to spread the money available over a number of years. In August 1972 with Stage 1 completed the *Cumberland News* reported "the Inner ring Road, when completed, should free the central area of Carlisle from traffic congestion". The demolition of a considerable number of houses in Denton Holme was to prove controversial and while some of the route was cleared remaining property on Milbourne Street was spared while a review was carried out. Common sense prevailed and the scheme was scrapped in the late 1970s.

Above: work in progress on the demolition of Charlotte Street in February 1977.

Right: demolition of Elm Street in 1977 where there were plans for a Ring Road roundabout.

DEMOLITION & REGENERATION

THE SLUMS OF CARLISLE

This is Denton Crescent, Carlisle. The houses have been condemned for over a year. nothing has been done to rehouse the tenants. Now they are petitioning the City Council action. The full story is one Page One

Carlisle Journal 7 July 1961

Left: the council policy before 1969 was to compulsorily purchase older property and demolish under slum clearance orders. Certain streets in Denton Holme suffered especially Denton Crescent, seen here before demolition with a suitable headline. The remainder of Denton Crescent was demolished in 1976 and 1977 in advance of the Inner Ring Road roundabout which was never built.

Cumbria County Council

Cumbria County Council

Denton Holme Survey 2013

The Denton Holme Survey was delivered to households in the Denton Holme Electoral Division to ask them what they felt about the area, what they liked and what could be improved

Carlisle Library

Between 1969 and 1974 Housing Acts recognised the important role which old houses perform in "meeting the demands of the lower end of the housing market" while recognising "the social advantage of keeping neighbourhoods together". Also avoided was "the need for cash programmes of redevelopment" by creating General Improvement Areas and Housing Action areas which attracted government grants.

In an April 1978 Council Housing Strategy Position Statement was identified "the largest concentration of unfit and substandard housing in Carlisle....is in Denton Holme.

This led to the creation of Housing Action Areas in Denton Holme in 1979. In reports produced as a result it was accepted "demolition is only recommended after very careful consideration". Where there had been demolition council flats were built to fill the gaps.

Denis Perriam two images

Above top: consultation documents now ensure that Denton Holme residents have a say in future planning issues.

Above: council flats on Lewis Court completed in 1979.

Left: demolition in Cumberland Street in 1975 to make way for Cumberland Court council flats which had been planned as early as 1967.

TELEVISION & FILM

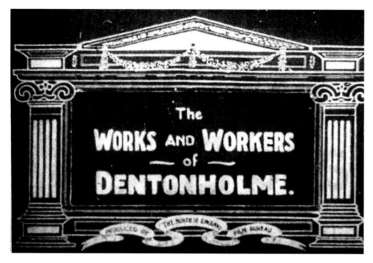

Above: the title for Leon Gould's film of 1910 which featured scenes in Lorne Crescent and the North Street entrance to Ferguson Bros.

Above: television put an end to the Rex Cinema which in 1962 was converted to a bingo hall.

Above: extras wait to take part in Mike Figgis' film in Colville Street North in 1999.

Above: in this 1958 view a TV aerial has been fitted to a Denton Holme house.

In the *Denton* magazine for 1964-5 C Johnston stated, "it was in August 1956 that our telly arrived. It took three men one day to assemble the aerial and secure it to the chimney". The TV did not work and the men had to come back and fit another aerial the next day.

Some or those who watched TV in the 1950s went on to a screen career. Eric Scott-Parker, born in Cumberland Street, became a TV cameraman. Roger Bolton, a Denton Holme schoolboy, became a TV presenter.

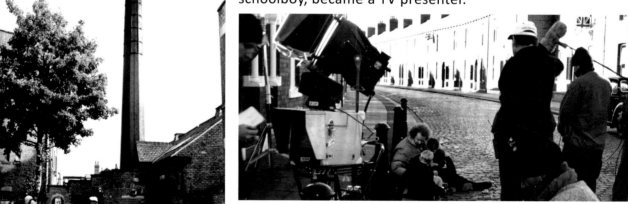

Above: cameras ready to roll in Colville Street for the film. Satellite dishes were disguised with Union Jacks.

Left: Oscar nominated director, Mike Figgis, [centre] was born in Carlisle and he came to shoot scenes in Denton Holme in 1999 for *The Loss of Sexual Innocence*, a film loosely based on his childhood. Central to these scenes was the Colville Street area and Teasdale's chimney in the background.

THEN AND NOW

Denis Perriam, all images.

Then: Viaduct Buildings at the corner of Randall Street and Charlotte Street.

Now: since 1976 demolition the site has remained an open space.

Then: looking along Charlotte Street to the Viaduct during 1976 demolition.

Now: some of the housing was replaced in 1979.

Then: preparation to demolish the Canal Branch bridge over Denton Street in 1974.

Now: no trace today that there had ever been a railway here.

THEN AND NOW

David Young

Then: Richardson Street looking from Frederick Street towards Norfolk Street before World War One. Smoke issues from Carrick's chimney and two boys play on the pavement.

Now: the housing is still all there. The only difference is the number of parked cars.

Denis Perriam

Then: Lorne Street in 1912 looking towards Denton Hill Works on Lorne Crescent

Now: houses on the left have been replaced by a modern building and some of the factory buildings have gone.

Cumberland News

Findlay Stirling, three images

Then: looking over the Dalston Road level crossing in 1966 towards Shaddongate.

Now: the level crossing and signal box have gone along with the railway and there are a number of new buildings along a widened street.

THEN AND NOW

Then: Denton Crescent during demolition in 1977 with the corner of Nelson Bridge Inn.

Denis Perriam, all images.

Now: the buildings have been replaced by gardens.

Then: Elm Street immediately before demolition in 1977.

Now: the same gardens as above cover the site.

Then: the corner of Junction Street and Shaddongate with Penningtons barbers shop on the angle in the late 1950s.

Now: the corner buildings were demolished being replaced by Willow's Garage in 1966. More recently this has become a base for a car hire firm.

THEN AND NOW

Then: the Avoiding Goods Lines are crossing the bridge over the Caldew and tracks on the left lead into the Denton Holme goods yard looking north west.

Now: the Avoiding Goods has become a riverside cycle track over the former railway bridge while the goods yard is now an industrial estate.

Then: Randall Street housing which had survived the building of the Victoria Viaduct.

Now: the housing on both sides of the street came down in advance of the Inner Ring Road scheme.

Denis Perriam, two images.

Findlay Stirling, three images.

Then: Denton Holme goods warehouse and yard when in use by Excel.

Now: all of the former railway buildings have been demolished to be replaced by the Lidl store and car park.

THEN AND NOW

Then: Norfolk Street and Cumberland Street during the 1975 demolition.

Now: replaced by social housing.

Then: Cumberland Street with Morley Street School in the distance.

Now: gone are the terraced houses and the school to be replaced with new housing.

Then: North Street in the Edwardian period with entrance gates into Ferguson Bros factory.

Now: the street survives with some modifications.

109

THEN AND NOW

Then: riverside fencing along the Caldew.

Now: a riverside path behind a flood wall.

Then: Canal Branch bridge over the Caldew during 1974 demolition.

Now: all that remains is part of the bridge pier in the river bed.

Then: Lime Street in the 1970s with terraced housing on both sides.

Now: housing on the left side of the street has been replaced by flats.

THEN AND NOW

Then: during filming in Colville Terrace in 1999 when it was a cul-de-sac.

Now: the former factory building has been replaced by houses along with a new street Holstead Close.

Then: Gilliland's shop on the corner of Colville Terrace and Colville Street in the 1950s.

Now: the shop converted to a private house.

Then: woodcut view over Murrell Hill showing the Morton Sundour property in 1951.

Now: the view from Nelson Street in the same direction.

OTHER LOCAL BOOKS AVAILABLE FROM P3 PUBLICATIONS

Title	ISBN	First published
Who Was Anne Gregg?	978-0-9931835-8-4	February 2019
Longtown Memories of Yesteryear	978-0-9931835-6-0	November 2018
Carlisle Suburbs Series: Stanwix	978-0-9931835-5-3	October 2018
Walks Around the Lorton Valley	978-0-9931835-4-6	May 2018
Botcherby - A Garden Village	978-0-9931835-2-2	May 2017
Carlisle's First Learning Centre: Tullie House	978-0-9934889-0-0	Spring 2016
The Carlisle Floods (2015), (with recollections from 2005)	978-0-9934889-1-7	December 2015
Allonby, A Short History and Guide	978-0-9572412-7-5	Spring 2014
Cumbrian Ancestors Unwrapped	978-0-9572412-6-8	Spring 2014
The Carlisle Ship Canal	978-0-9572412-4-4	October 2013
A Century Around Silloth	978-0-9572412-3-7	October2012
Chanel and the Tweedmaker, Weavers of Dreams	978-0-9572412-2-0	September 2012
Watching over Carlisle, 140 years of the Carlisle City Police (1827-1967)	978-0-9559017-6-8	July 2011

For more books and further details go to **http://www.p3publications.com**
Books can be purchased online using Paypal or credit/debit card

FORTHCOMING IN THIS SERIES

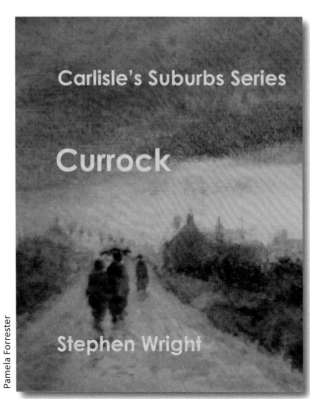